Everything Runs Like a Movie

EVERYTHING RUNS LIKE A MOVIE

The Strange but True Story of
Bank Robber Hermann Beier

JOHN COOPER

DUNDURN
TORONTO

Editor: Allison Hirst
Design: Courtney Horner
Printer: Webcom

Library and Archives Canada Cataloguing in Publication

Cooper, John, 1958-

   Everything runs like a movie : the strange but true story of bank robber Hermann Beier / John Cooper.

Issued also in electronic formats.
ISBN 978-1-4597-0829-7

   1. Beier, Hermann. 2. Brigands and robbers--Ontario--Biography. 3. Bank robberies--Ontario. I. Title.

HV6653.B45C66 2013   364.15'52092   C2013-900785-7

1 2 3 4 5   17 16 15 14 13

Conseil des Arts du Canada Canada Council for the Arts

Canada

ONTARIO ARTS COUNCIL
CONSEIL DES ARTS DE L'ONTARIO

We acknowledge the support of the **Canada Council for the Arts** and the **Ontario Arts Council** for our publishing program. We also acknowledge the financial support of the **Government of Canada** through the **Canada Book Fund** and **Livres Canada Books**, and the **Government of Ontario** through the **Ontario Book Publishing Tax Credit** and the **Ontario Media Development Corporation**.

Care has been taken to trace the ownership of copyright material used in this book. The author and the publisher welcome any information enabling them to rectify any references or credits in subsequent editions.

J. Kirk Howard, President

Printed and bound in Canada.

Visit us at
Dundurn.com
Definingcanada.ca
@dundurnpress
Facebook.com/dundurnpress

Dundurn
3 Church Street, Suite 500
Toronto, Ontario, Canada
M5E 1M2

Gazelle Book Services Limited
White Cross Mills
High Town, Lancaster, England
LA1 4XS

Dundurn
2250 Military Road
Tonawanda, NY
U.S.A. 14150

For my sons,
Tyler and Cole Cooper,
and my granddaughter,
McKenna Bevan

The names of some individuals have
been changed to protect their identities.

CONTENTS

ACKNOWLEDGEMENTS

WRITING A BOOK THAT SPANS TWENTY YEARS CANNOT BE DONE WITHOUT the support of a great number of people, individuals who give freely of their knowledge, expertise, guidance, and enthusiasm. To that end, I offer my thanks to the following people and organizations for their assistance and support: my agent, Bill Hanna; my editor at Dundurn Press, Allison Hirst; Allan Dickie; Jerry Amernic; the late author Brian Vallée (who read an early version of the manuscript and liked what he saw); the Halton Regional Police Service; the Guelph Police Service; the Ontario Provincial Police; the Correctional Service of Canada; the staff at the Alliston Public Library and Whitby Public Library; the Royal Bank of Canada and its employees, especially those who willingly recounted to me their stories about the robberies; and the staff at Millhaven, Collins Bay, and Joyceville penitentiaries, as well as staff at the Toronto East and West Detention Centres. And last, my sincere thanks go out to Paul Stern, Paula Beard, and James Carlisle.

1

Desperado

For Hermann Beier, the beginning of the end started on the morning of October 30, 1991, with a call placed to a limousine company. It ended on Halloween day, against a fence in a vacant field, in a flurry of police bullets, a scene worthy of a Brian de Palma film or an Elmore Leonard novel.

For me, the story began on February 17, 1993. That was the day the *Toronto Star* ran a story about a bird breeder from the town of Alliston, Ontario, who had been sentenced to thirteen years in prison. "Hermann Hans Beier, 51, was caught October 31, 1991, after leading three police forces on a wild, gun-firing chase from Guelph to Caledon in a hijacked airport limousine he'd used in five bank holdups," the *Star*'s Farrell Crook wrote.

I read the story with surprise. Could this be the same Hermann Beier who used to live in Kleinburg? The same man who raised budgies? The genial, fun-loving guy who had his own business — Hermann the Handyman? Was this the same guy I had written about eight years earlier for a community newspaper?

It was. As Crook wrote in the *Star*, "Beier 'will be an old man when the sentence expires,' the judge [Justice Kenneth Langdon of Ontario Court, General Division] said during sentencing."

The question for me was: How did this happen? And more importantly, why?

§

Hermann Beier was portrayed as a desperado, a bank robber speeding from the law in a stolen Lincoln Town Car, racing along concession roads between Guelph and Caledon at 160 kilometres an hour. Over the course of 120 kilometres of sleepy back-country road, he tossed smoke bombs out of the window of the limo at the fifteen cars from four different police forces pursuing him. He screeched to a stop at intersections, leaping from his car to exchange gunfire with police. All the time, an Ontario Provincial Police helicopter buzzed overhead. It was the biggest police chase in Ontario history and possibly the biggest in Canada at the time.

Beier was packing three loaded guns that outclassed anything the police had to use against him. A .22 handgun, a .44 Magnum, and a .357 Magnum sat on the passenger seat beside bags of money stolen from Royal Bank branches in Georgetown, Rockwood, and Guelph. Jamming to a halt and leaping from the car to exchange gunfire, Hermann was a deadly comic figure dressed in a black ninja-style outfit; like a warrior from a war-torn country, he sported bullet belts across his chest. He was imposing enough that officers initially reported him to be at least six feet tall, a full five inches taller than his actual height. He was bull-chested, and his silver hair was puffed out like a caricature — the vision was that of a gentle clown gone stark raving mad.

But the reality on that sunny afternoon was just too stark, too cruel for the gentle rural countryside. The smell of burning rubber and the sight of overheated cars and frantic exchanges between cops anxious to end the chase were too visceral for just a Halloween prank gone awry. From the police helicopters, the cruisers looked like a stream of metal boxes tearing through the farming communities, pounding along the grit and the gravel of highways that cut neatly through cornfields and past snug brick two-storey homes trimmed in white. It was a cold and calculated event planned by a desperate man, a man whose dreams evaporated as quickly as drops of water after a desert rainfall. Police later discovered in the car a list of twenty-five banks and trust companies, along with plans to rob each in succession. It was a textbook plan, followed to the letter but cut short before its completion.

The chain of events began and ended with guns: a gun to the head of a Punjabi-speaking limousine driver at a Toronto airport hotel; a gun pointed at frightened bank tellers, accompanied by terse German-accented commands to fill several grocery bags with money. On country roads, handguns wielded by the fleeing bank robber blazed away at pursuing police officers. In the end, a standard-issue police revolver felled Hermann Beier.

The day was loaded with a succession of events, capsules of intense violence compacted into the time-space of seconds. Hermann, sweating, seeing nothing but the dusty road in front of him, jumped from the car to unload endless rounds of firecracker lead. The cops fired back, giving up on the idea of trying to end the chase quietly. It was a cycle that repeated itself several times. It seemed as if it would never end.

On October 31, 1991, Hermann Beier's life as a private citizen ended in a way only fitting for a desperado; with six bullet wounds in his left leg and hip, he lay slumped over in a dirty culvert beside a dusty side road in a no man's land northwest of Toronto.

Later, more than 120 charges were filed against him, including the attempted murder of thirteen police officers.

In the end, a total of $134,000 from the robbery of five banks and a trust company in six different towns had been stolen — and not all of the money was recovered.

Officers who were involved in the chase that day were left shaken and nervous, trying to cope with the intensity of the event. It was a day that remained indelibly etched in their memories, and, as far as excitement goes, the apex of several careers.

Hermann Beier, fifty-one years of age at the time, was later sentenced to thirteen years in prison. The Crown appealed the sentence as too light, not enough, they said, for a desperado of Hermann's calibre. Countering these efforts was Hermann's lawyer, who fought for a shorter sentence, citing Hermann's lack of a previous criminal record.

§

On the second to last day in March 1993, Hermann Beier sat in a cramped office at Millhaven Penitentiary in Bath, Ontario. For a shorter man, he was big — he had sinewy arms, a thick chest, and broad hands that were leathery from years of renovation work and carpentry. A round belly that couldn't quite hide behind the line of his belt seemed to have a robust strength to it. He had dangerous eyes, suspicious and questioning.

His accent was big, too, thick and Teutonic. It rolled around in his mouth and spilled out in heavy droplets. His hair was thinning and silvery, but on the sides it was thick and wavy. Hermann didn't smile a lot; there wasn't a lot *to* smile about there. When he did smile, the creases around his eyes were deep.

Hermann worked hard to carry himself like a younger man. But he wasn't. He was half a century old and feeling his age. When he was finally free again, he would be an old man.

None of this made sense to me at the time. Despite his visage, this was a gentle man as I remembered him; a kind, sweet man who took care of budgies, for God's sake. A man who loved people, loved animals, hired kids as apprentices for his handyman company, got involved in the community, raised dogs and prize-winning birds, taught martial arts, and chatted with small-town police officers in the local doughnut shop.

This was not your typical bank robber. So why was he behind bars?

2

Hermann the Handyman, 1985

Imagine a clean, white clapboard farmhouse sitting on a rise of property that falls away to reveal green fields all around. In 1985, I visited this farmhouse in the Kleinburg area. I drove along a dusty concession road, then up a dirt driveway for about two hundred metres.

A stocky man with thinning, greying hair and a big smile met me at the door. He was about five foot seven. Reaching out to me with a thick worker's hand, his calloused fingers tightly gripped my embarrassingly smooth palm. He wore work pants that were soiled and stained. They were threadbare in spots, with blotches of paint here and there, as if to prove that this was a man who earned his keep, the son of strong German stock who knew what it was like to work for a day's wage. A golf shirt stretched across his chest, grey hairs peeking out from the neckline.

Hermann's voice seemed as thick as his hands, heady like German brew. It roiled and bubbled with happiness, ready to explain to anyone that he was a man — a *man's man* — making a go of it here in Canada. He referred to his adopted country often in our talk, of the Canada that beckoned to him with its open lands and blue skies, a land not obfuscated and darkened by soot, not cut and sliced into sections by the visual pollution of wires and antennae, or poisoned by the vestiges of racial hatred.

This land to him was New with a capital *N*, and it carried a heavy weight of meaning for him because of what it represented: a break from the past and a chance to start fresh after many previous disappointments in his life. It was here that a man could be reborn, he thought. Here he could shed everything that he was and become someone new. Here he could emulate his movie heroes, people like Clint Eastwood, keeping evil at bay with a .44 Magnum, or like Bruce Lee and Jean Claude Van Damme, and (real or imagined) chop-sockying the bad guys into oblivion. He felt this was a country where everyone was promised a new start. He could reinvent himself, using the discipline gained from his upbringing, and forge a new life.

Across the lawn was a great moving bundle of grey and white, a knot of rubber-jointed sheepdogs, happy in a foolhardy puppy way, bounding around the property, looking like overgrown cartoon dogs newly escaped from the celluloid.

We entered the house via a side door. This led into an anteroom that opened into a kitchen, with high ceilings like other farmhouses in the area. The room was warmed by its southern exposure to the afternoon sun. The living room boasted a large fireplace, a few sticks of furniture, a well-worn sofa, and little else save for a smattering of books. An ambience of well-worn memories from the early years of this century — haying, harvesting, tending livestock — hung in the air, as thick and rich and Canadian as sizzling back bacon. To Hermann Beier, it was home. It was New. And he was being reborn.

He proudly showed me what he was doing to fix up the place — replacing cupboards, fixing the floor, repairing a doorway. This tour of Hermann's handyman skills served merely to frame his real passion, his birds, scores of them, velvet colours taking flight in roomy, scrupulously clean flight cages. They were like animated figures from cels of Disney cartoons given three-dimensional life.

I had arrived that day to talk to him about his birds. Hermann had called my editor earlier in the week and they had discussed his plans to start a bird sanctuary.

Like every other community newspaper, the *Liberal*'s editorial livelihood focused on the community — its people and historical stories and events, from strawberry socials to the Kleinburg Binder Twine Festival. Hermann's was just another in the stream of faces, brightly lit with ideas and dreams that played out against a neighbourhood whose landscape was rapidly changing from rural to suburban as new subdivisions gorged themselves on the farm-

Photo by John Cooper

Hermann in a 1985 news photo showing off one of his prize harlequin budgies. He had big plans to set up a bird sanctuary in York Region, as well as a kennel to raise and sell Old English sheepdogs.

land. My editor, Marney Beck, thirty years old, a bright-eyed, long-limbed believer in small towns, loved the idea of a feature on Hermann.

"The girl," was how Hermann referred to Marney when I spoke with him over the phone. I reminded him that she was my editor, my boss. "She sounds like a nice girl," he repeated. "I like the fact that she speaks some German."

From the rise of land where the farmhouse perched, I could see the change in the view as I looked from west to east, the sprawl of Metro Toronto creeping north, a strange octopus-like animal by the lake, stretching its many arms, the subdivisions flowing into them with ease and finally filling in the gaps between the tentacles. I could see as I shifted my gaze how the suburb reproduced itself in orderly, mathematically precise little squares of grey and black and brown, establishing strongholds in Woodbridge, Thornhill, and Richmond Hill.

Hermann Beier, in front of his wall of winning ribbons, at his Kleinburg farmhouse.
He worked as a handyman, budgie breeder, and martial arts trainer.

But inside that farmhouse, I felt safe from that. I sipped coffee against a curtain of budgie sounds and budgie colours, a busy chattering and blurry *wuzz-wuzzing* of wings as the birds moved from perch to perch, shifting in a crazy paint-rag quilt of pastel shades, heads bobbing up and down. I felt the sharp pang of budgie doo-doo in my nose as I turned to look out at farm fields that lay in a happy, lazy season of fallow. Toronto seemed a hundred miles, a hundred years, away.

And there was Hermann's face, lit by the late afternoon sun as he talked to me in a chop-chop staccato of German-accented English. His comments were punctuated by a sense of hope, all those percussive words that came accompanied by rim-shots and cymbal crashes of desire, raw desire. Everything he told me was underscored by the short and pithy words "I want to do this. I have to do this. I really *will* do this."

His goal was to make his *ideal self* a reality — to have a high profile, fame, and fortune. To be *somebody*. He was anxious to make his mark, afraid perhaps that if he didn't, he would end up like so many others, accepting drudgery as the norm, slipping into a banal and placid life, becoming self-limiting and giving up on his goals.

His desire to break the chains imposed by family, society, and even his own self-doubt, drove him to succeed. When Hermann grasped the second chance that freedom in Canada represented, he wasn't about to accept any limitations. Reaching his goals would fulfil his desire to be free, both physically and mentally.

3

Millhaven Penitentiary, March 1993

Although it is often associated with the city of Kingston, Ontario, Millhaven Penitentiary, a maximum security institution, is actually in the village of Bath, about twenty kilometres to the west. To get to it from Highway 401, you travel along Highway 33, which hugs the north shore of Lake Ontario. A big sign announces the entrance to Millhaven and the medium security Bath Institution with which it shares the property.

There was plenty of time for me to wonder about the look of Millhaven as I drove up and around the curving road that led to the front entrance. The grass was crisp-looking, brown after a hard winter, and patches of old snow melted slowly in the late winter sun. Collections of granite boulders and densely planted thickets of evergreens were grouped in seemingly random fashion on the landscaped property, breaking up the gently rolling fields.

As I approached, I saw a series of long, low buildings. Men in plain blue pants and light-blue shirts, a handful of them, stood around outside. One of them, a young guy with a scrubby beard and straggly, dirty, shoulder-length blond hair moved a rake, not too convincingly, over a small pile of dried-up grass and twigs. "Is this Millhaven?" I asked him, assuming I was somewhere on the grounds.

The young man chuckled. "That's over there," he said, with a wave of his hand. I couldn't follow it. The wave was too blasé, too noncommittal. Then, as if he had sensed my lack of understanding, he added, "Go to the end of the road, and where it goes into a fork in the road, go to the right."

The buildings that were in sight comprised the Bath Institution. And these men were inmates of that facility, where they would have greater privileges than their counterparts at Millhaven. They would have the freedom to move about outside, for instance, to breathe the fresh air and feel the sunshine on their faces. Not so at Millhaven, an institution that has a reputation as the toughest penitentiary in the country, a place of mayhem and sometimes murder.

Sure enough, I travelled down the road, took the right fork, and there it was, like something out of a prison movie — tall guard towers, double fences, razor wire, and gravel expanses. One lone cramped box of a building, the entrance to the institution, was crouched beneath one of the guard towers. I parked and entered the building, and after providing identification, having my personal possessions searched, and passing through a metal detector, I was finally allowed entrance. Though I hadn't asked about the procedure, the guard offered an explanation: "It makes no difference who you are," he said, not unkindly, "[it's the] same for everybody."

He was a tall, lean guy in his early fifties, friendly and cooperative. He asked me to sign in. Although he leaned forward on the counter, like a country shopkeeper ready to tell me about goings-on in this neck of the woods, he just smiled and watched me sign my name. I exited the opposite side of the building and walked down a path until I stood in front of a ten-metre-high gate. Someone, somewhere, pushed a button and the gate creaked and cranked, then slid back to let me through. I was in no man's land, a six-metre gap between the two soaring fences. On either side, beyond the chain link, white gravel swept around the perimeter of the facility. I waited, ten, twenty seconds, and then heard a short buzzing sound. The second gate opened. I was now on the grounds, walking between low white buildings that reminded me of the schoolyard portable classrooms of my childhood. An inmate was planting flowers — red geraniums, white petunias — in the rich soil of the flowerbeds outside the entrance to the main building.

Millhaven Penitentiary has a grim, foreboding look worthy of a prison movie, with ominous razor wire, soaring fences, and guard towers. The atmosphere is no different inside.

The grounds were as imposing as I expected: ten-metre-high double fences topped with razor wire; guard towers; warning fences in the exercise yard (try to scale these, and the guards will use whatever force is necessary to stop you); three units (each with two levels) that housed four hundred inmates; a unit for segregation; and a hospital. The building was slate grey, and although carefully planned and built, from a distance it looked like series of randomly arranged giant children's blocks — slabs of concrete arranged here and there; one block looked as if it had been added as an afterthought. In aerial photos, it is a thing of stark architectural beauty, its passageways and courtyards forming a trillium shape buttressed by concrete, and geometrically defined by steel and gravel. Opened in 1971, the facility was built in a way to maximize control, minimize uncertainty, and limit the personal freedom of its inmates

Hermann Beier's case worker met me inside. She was friendly, smiling, and offered a firm handshake. After exchanging a few pleasantries, she led me down a long hallway, the two sides of the corridor separated by heavy-duty chicken-wire-style blue mesh. This led to a sizeable atrium, where several hallways branched off in different directions. I was directed to follow the signs and headed toward the work range, the case worker leading the way. There we were met by a beefy red-haired chief-of-guards kind of guy — he declined to give me his official title — and a couple of his subordinates. When you visit a penitentiary, the security and control is inherent and dominating — the feeling of control pulses like a steady heartbeat throughout the place. Once your identity has been checked and rechecked, you are handed off from one official to the other, in my case from case worker to guard. The chief-of-guards was a character built for this environment, with his heavy, rounded shoulders, nasty little eyes, and thick hands that looked dry and rough. The office he led me into was about four metres long, but felt very cramped.

I was told to wait in the office. A female guard, short and strongly built, with brown curls that bubbled up to frame an appealing face, waited with me. Talkative, she smiled as she made pleasant conversation, inquiring as to whom I was visiting. She revealed to me that she was a country and western singer and about to cut her first record. I asked if Millhaven was a good place to get inspiration for her songs, seeing as how, as with most country songs, they must be about hurtin' and stuff like that. She gave me an odd look, as if trying to figure out whether or not I was putting her on. "There's a lot of pain here," she said, suddenly serious.

An inmate was working in the guards' office. His face was pock-marked with acne scars and his jet-black hair framed large and curious eyes set above a Roman nose and drooping black moustache. He leaned back in his chair, holding a clipboard in his hand: "So, you're writing about Beier? Gonna get this on the AP? Gonna get this on the wire?"

He said it loudly, too loudly, emphasizing the words. "*I know about the wire.*" What does he know about wire stories? What is the significance? I told him I was trying to write a book. "Yup," he said and his eyes pierced me. "Gonna get this one *on the wire.*" I was a bit slow on the uptake, not realizing that this guy didn't want conversation, only agreement. He wanted someone to give affirmation to his comment. "Yes," I lied, "maybe this will get on the wire."

Why did I lie, I asked myself? Why didn't I get into a conversation? Because, as I discovered much later, you didn't do that there. In Millhaven, things either *are* or they're *not*. There is no room for anything between.

§

There wasn't a lot of time to ponder this question, because Hermann arrived at that moment for our interview. The conversation took place in a cramped interview room used by social workers, lawyers, clergy, and other visitors. He wore blue jeans and a casual shirt, and a black plastic crucifix and rosary were draped around his neck, the cross nestled prominently in the vee of his open-necked shirt. His hair was silvery grey and long. If he was going for the look of a hip, aging artist, he had hit his target. The look was convincing.

During that first conversation, Hermann was sometimes hesitant, sometimes passionate; he thumped his thick fingers into the palm of his hand for emphasis. He would periodically look out through the louvred blinds into the enclosed courtyard and his eyes would narrow. Sometimes he leaned back in his chair, searching for the right words in English to express himself. "I know what I want to say, but it's easier in German than English," was a frequent comment. Occasionally his eyes were moist, especially when he spoke to me about his former girlfriends.

We talked for almost three hours. We had to take a break after about an hour, when a terse social worker demanded use of the interview room. Except for a few individuals whose good nature stood out glaringly under the circumstances, just about everyone there that day — guards, social workers, office staff, inmates — was edgy, temperamental, tense, and abrupt. Everyone, it seemed, had something they were waiting for: the end of the day, an interview, meals, parole. It was just the course of things there. Smiles were rare, and regimentation the norm.

After the interruption, we resumed our conversation in a second-floor meeting room that was decorated with Native artwork — sweeping, grand lines painted over the glossy yellow brick.

Hermann explained how one of his former girlfriends had helped him get started in the renovation business: "She gave me the name, she found a name that's interesting or funny or whatever, Hermann the Handyman, and I built this business up with her help because she was well known in Ontario. She had her own business, two businesses [actually]. In one business she was consulting, in telemarketing. At the time, she had just sold [that business]. She was in real estate. She had her own business and she had a lot of money, but I didn't know it at the time. Anyway, the money was not important. What *was* important [was that] she helped me to get jobs.

"Somehow our relationship broke for some reason ... well, I feel sorry today, for quite a while already, because when you come from Europe you have one major feeling or attitude. When you come from Europe or are German, you feel that certain things have to have certain places. I'm an organized person. My house was pretty clean. She was a wonderful woman, a lovable person, but not organized. She would come home and she would drop the clothes somewhere, in the corner. Lots of Canadian or North American people are like that. In my life, when I was doing renovations or renting houses or apartments, I saw this [behaviour] everywhere. I'm disappointed in one way for me, but this is how North American people sometimes live." But he could ignore the sloppiness of Canadians; he was focused on setting and achieving his goals, which included making money. In order to make ends meet, he got a job at a nursing home.

"I had this job; it was a part-time job, in a nursing home in Kleinburg, because in the wintertime I had no jobs in renovations, so I took this part-time job."

He worked there only five hours a day, which allowed him to go off to renovation jobs as they became available. He was friendly, affable, and he loved to help people.

The budgie breeding took off for him at that time also, and Hermann became a champion breeder and a judge at shows, earning a measure of respect in budgie breeding circles. "I got mail from around the world. I ... started to [write] for *Budgerigar World* newspaper in England. This newspaper goes around the world."

Still, his experiences in Kleinburg were not always positive. At first it seemed that everything would go the way he wanted it to: Orderly. Efficient. Focused. He had a five-year deal to rent a big roomy farmhouse that sat on an elevated piece of farmland.

It was quiet, isolated, and very rustic. A patchwork quilt of green fields spread out around the farmhouse. While it wasn't in the best shape, the farmhouse was liveable, and Hermann had a deal with his landlord to fix it up in exchange for a reduction in the rent. Bringing it up to acceptable standards took him three years, he says.

It was a place where he could finally raise budgies and sheepdogs. It would also serve as a home for the bird sanctuary that he planned to eventually open. Over time, he put together a clean-lined aviary of wood and wire, and he said he was pleased with the final design.

But problems loomed. The winter of 1985–86 was particularly bitter and Hermann was at odds with Ontario Hydro. He explained to me what happened.

"Twice [it] happened … in the winter time or the beginning of spring. A big tree that I had in the front of the house broke my hydro [line]. It took the hydro days to come to my place to fix it." The electrical heaters in the bird room failed. It was a crisis of major proportions, because the budgies, and especially their newborns, needed constant warmth. Hermann said he would have done anything to keep his birds warm.

"One time, my girlfriend Joanne came to visit me and she found me lying in the bird room, totally drunk. She never saw me drunk before or after … but I was totally drunk because I was drinking to keep me warm. I lay down in my birds' room to keep the birds warm. I had no electricity; my furnace would not jump up because I had no hydro."

On a more personal level, Hermann was also upset and depressed about his current relationship. Hydro plus cold budgies plus relationship issues equalled his first major crisis in Canada.

Even in a prison meeting room years later, Hermann was still dwelling on the Hydro situation. Though it had happened more than seven years earlier, and his problems were now much more serious, he still felt slighted by the dispute with the utility.

"I don't have any more proof about this because … some papers disappeared," he added.

The bird sanctuary would also become the focal point of a second major incident.

He was proud of the bird sanctuary. As ideas went, it had been a good one. As designer, builder, and promoter, Hermann carried the project off well. He used his handyman skills to put up a wood and chicken-wire enclosure and stocked it with pheasants, peacocks, rare black swans, and other birds, along with some goats. There was interest from the local media, and Hermann thrived on the attention he received during and after the official opening of the sanctuary by Vaughan mayor Lorna

Jackson. It became a popular site for classroom visits, and interested members of the public also stopped by just to take a look. For Hermann, the sanctuary provided a cultural connection to his homeland, where well-made, well-run zoos had been a tradition for hundreds of years, and where animal conservation was popular. Hermann openly admitted to me that he loved the attention. During the interview, he repeated several times that he saw it as his opportunity to educate the public about birds and about conservation.

"Until one day," he said, rubbing his hand against his temple, his accent thick and rough in his throat, "somebody came up [there] and killed all my birds ... they got the wire open.... This girl that I hired to watch the birds when I was [away] in the daytime working, she called me up and told me, 'Hermann, come home.'"

The police were already there when Hermann arrived. He was bitterly disappointed with what he alleges as police inaction. *Why didn't they care about his birds?* he wondered. He told me the policeman said it must have been an animal that killed his birds — a dog or a coyote perhaps. Hermann looked down at the floor as he told me this. "Yeah, an animal *on two legs*, because the way it [the wire mesh] was ... balled up, folded up from the bottom, wrapped up. No animal does that." He believed it could only have been a person.

He explained that whoever opened the mesh either killed the animals themselves or set loose a couple of dogs into the compound. "And this person, or who[ever] was there, one or two of the dogs, I don't know, killed the animals, the goats, the pheasant, the chickens." Two or three pigeons still winged frantically around the enclosure, "but," he told me, "the rest of the bigger animals were all dead. And the worst part was the black swans ... [someone] cut off the heads, a really nice clean cut."

His anger at the police bubbled up again. "The police didn't do anything at all. I always was [angry] and still I respect the police because without police a country cannot live. You have to have rules, but I was disappointed he [the police officer] didn't do anything."

Hermann believed there were several people determined to ruin his business and his bird sanctuary. But he wouldn't elaborate. "People started screwing me up."

It was at this point that he told me about his ex-roommate, Chris. This was the first time he had mentioned a roommate, and he told me that the man had been more than a bit odd. He owned a large German shepherd, and was thought to be a suspect in the deaths of Hermann's menagerie, but the police never pursued that angle. "This man, for example, he tapped my phone. He listened to all my phone conversations. I finally called the police, [but] they did not do anything."

I asked Hermann if he ever got into a physical fight with Chris. His eyebrows pulled down low over his eyes and he scowled: "I never touched him. I warned him a few times." He assured me he was always a peaceful man.

But Hermann felt Chris was a problem, not only because he was a snoop, but because he thought of him as a threat to his relationships: Hermann was as possessive of his women as he was of his budgies. He told me the roommate had made several passes at his girlfriend at the time. And Chris was also very close, a little *too close* perhaps, to his dog, which bothered Hermann.

"The worst part was one time I finally freaked out. I come home from work and I caught him in the shower with his dog. He showered with his dog in my shower! A big German shepherd." Hermann had never seen anything like it. "I said, finally, 'that's enough. Now make sure you go out.' So, he said, 'You have to give me a notice.' That's what I did, and still he did not move out. So, anyway, finally he moved out sometime in January."

He also cleaned out the place, Hermann told me, taking several of Hermann's personal items: "I filed a [police] report, but they did not find him."

Hermann considered the former roommate and his dog prime suspects in the killing of the sanctuary's birds. "I believe afterward maybe he did it because he wanted to get even with me. There was no investigation. I mean, I'm not talking about the money that I lost. About five or six thousand dollars I lost, except I built all the cages, all that I paid [for]. That's just not the point. I lost a lot of money, but that's just not the point. The point is the animals. The animals, in all my life animals were very important to me. I love animals, especially dogs and birds."

Despite the conflict with Chris, Hermann said that things began to come together for him in a positive way after he got deeper into his relationship with Joanne.

"We decided to buy a house in Tottenham. South of Tottenham, south of Highway 9. I had at this time a Cadillac, because in Germany I always had a small car. Finally, I said 'I live in North America, now I'm going to enjoy my dream. I want to have a big car. I have just one life, so enjoy it.' So, I buy a Cadillac Seville — four doors, a nice car. But my dream car was always a Cadillac Eldorado, sporty looking, a big car, but sporty looking. I bought an Eldorado, fixed it up, spent some money on this car to fix it up."

The Eldorado was a '78 — "the last big one," Hermann says with pride. It was royal blue. The car had tinted glass, custom-made rims, and a car phone that Hermann used to conduct business. Hermann said the police homed in on him when he drove it. "From [that] moment ... wherever I drove, the police were steady behind me." The assumption was that they suspected him of criminal activity.

By this time, he said, the renovation business was moving along well. True to the name of the company, he did a bit of everything: "We built decks, in cottage country we fixed cottages, painted, or whatever."

Hermann worked hard. He said that despite their occasional bouts of slovenliness, Canadians were focused on work, especially those involved in the trades. He began to realize that if he could incorporate his company, he would get tax breaks, could apply to hire apprentices, and his legal liabilities would be limited. It was the Canadian business dream, and so, he told me, "I get the licence and make my company limited. So in the end I was allowed to teach young people, in an apprenticeship."

He loved taking on apprentices and enjoyed teaching them about the renovation business.

But he told me that throughout this period the police continued to hound him: "When I go off on the weekend out of the way or to customers, whatever, all of a sudden police car was behind me. And the police were steady behind me and when [they] stopped me [they were] surprised to see an old man sitting in the car. Not like a, well, I felt sometimes like a pimp or [drug] dealer. Sometimes he checked my car. I had nothing. Except sometimes I had loud music and at the time I liked reggae music. When I was by myself, it was a little bit loud. So people said that police are disappointed to find ordinary normal person. Sometime they would [say] 'sorry sir, Mr. Beier.' I was starting to get upset about it.

They were steady on the highway, on the streets, wherever I [was] … but this was not the point. The point was that I get more upset later …"

His frustration with the police began to build. Because of what he saw as their inaction in the bird sanctuary incident and the fact that he was being followed and stopped on suspicion of dealing drugs, Hermann was beginning to lose trust in the police and see them as a potential enemy. The alleged police harassment triggered greater stress in his increasingly stormy relationship with Joanne.

Joanne was a registered nurse who lived with Hermann from 1987 to 1989. The pair met at a nursing home in the Kleinburg area; they courted while Hermann lived in Kleinburg, and bought the Tottenham house together. When they broke up, they continued to see each other occasionally.

In a later phone interview, Joanne said "we were lovers for a while [after the breakup.]" She said this with a girlish giggle, as if she had broken the rules. In any case, she said, the pair had separated long before Hermann robbed his first bank.

She described Hermann as having a contradictory personality. "I think he liked to keep you guessing. He was passionate, yes, but extremely possessive. He still had old German values that men were the breadwinners and women were to be barefoot and pregnant in the kitchen."

Sparks flew between Hermann and Joanne's daughter, then twelve. "When we lived together, she was very rebellious and Hermann wanted to make her into a carbon copy of himself, only female."

Money was always an issue, she said. The pair took out a $40,000 second mortgage to keep the handyman business afloat in December of 1988; at the time of the interview, it was a mortgage Joanne said she was still paying off.

"He [really wanted] to make a go of the bird sanctuary [in Kleinburg]. He sacrificed safety for cost. We went to visit a Mrs. Innman, who ran a bird sanctuary in Mississauga. She knew his cages were not safe from attacks from wild animals."

Joanne didn't believe that it was a person who destroyed Hermann's birds: "I didn't think he had any enemies who would want to hurt him that way."

She also told me that Hermann had a mean streak that could come out in frightening ways. "One day I found two dead budgies on my counter and he accused my daughter [then thirteen] of giving them the 'evil eye.'" At the time, Hermann had a bank of twenty breeding boxes and a long flight pen. While no one, including Hermann, is sure of the exact number of budgies he kept, it was around a hundred, Masters said. It turned out that the two birds had died of a bacterial infection, detected after a lengthy autopsy at the University of Guelph. Hermann never apologized for his accusation, though, Joanne told me emphatically.

Hermann and Joanne never married. "We toyed with the idea, but we never did," said Joanne. "We took two lovely trips — to England in 1988 for an international budgie show in August, and to Germany in 1989 to visit his family."

Joanne described Hermann as a rebel and someone obsessed with being young: "If he knew someone who discovered the fountain of youth, he would be the first one to arrive."

I asked her what she thought Hermann's philosophy was. "He said 'I don't follow the rules. I make my own rules.'" She paused before continuing. "He loved me because I gave good back rubs. I don't know what I could have done to hold [onto] him. He was just a vagabond going from adventure to adventure. He was always going from lady to lady. I don't know how many times he might have fooled around on me."

When I mentioned this to Hermann in a later interview, he disagreed: "I [was] not jumping from one woman to another. I'm a one-woman man. If I have a girlfriend, I don't touch anybody else. I have a lot of women friends, but not as girlfriends."

After the relationship with Joanne ended, Hermann moved to Schomberg to get away from the situation. There, he met a new woman and had a brief "summer romance." He bluntly told me that her looks were his sole motivation. "She was a single woman. She told me she loved me or she was interested in me. I was not interested. I was only interested because she was a good-looking woman. I was single. I had no girlfriend. So, we had a one-summer friendship."

That relationship didn't last, and six months later he moved to Alliston — a town that he thought was, geographically, a great location for his business. "That was my dream. I was looking around to find a commercial place for my renovation business. Wherever I went, money was too much until I found a good place in Alliston. Then I realized that Alliston is exactly in the middle of what I expected [in terms of business prospects]. You have lots [of business] in Barrie, lots in Newmarket, lots in Orangeville, and you go south and it's Woodbridge. Alliston was exactly in the middle."

But Hermann had more ambitious plans. In addition to relocating his handyman business, he had made the decision to open a martial arts and fitness centre. This new and exciting project would help him to focus his energy. Hermann told me he had earned his black belt in Hapkido and that he was a third degree black belt. He said he taught the sport in Germany. The current trends of the day sent a clear message to him: if he started a martial arts centre, he would have women coming to him in droves to learn self-defence. And men in the community would follow, to get in shape.

"If you listen in the newspapers, in the media, whatever, women get attacked; there are lots of assaults, rapes, and so on. I [decided it was] not a bad idea to teach people, especially girls [and] women, to teach them martial arts, self-defence. I understood my business, so I found this place in Alliston on Dufferin Street South."

Hermann rented two units in a tiny plaza. "For renting two places I get a discount, and then I rented three places because I find out the place was not big enough. So, again I get discount. In two places that I rent I make the fitness centre and martial arts school and the third place for my renovations office." Soon another unit was added for his budgie operation, and he named the store Harlequin Place.

While living in a small apartment in Alliston, Hermann watched his businesses grow. "Nineteen eighty-nine was my biggest year. I had seven people working for me: three full-timers and four students in the summer-time. I was well-known in this area. Anyway, I opened my fitness centre [in March, 1990]. The mayor was there to open it up and everybody said it was a great idea and a great thing in Alliston that something like this could open up. In the daytime I was working in my renovations mostly, and in the evenings twice a week I started to teach martial arts. In 1990 [I had] lots of calls in the beginning of the year for renovations. Lots of people wanted to build decks, especially in the Alliston and Angus area."

However, when there was a downturn in the economy, Hermann found that his businesses were becoming liabilities. People began cancelling renovation work. Hermann sold one of his two vans. But the martial arts school, initially in serious debt, became a money-maker; it allowed Hermann to keep the three units going.

Courtesy of Hermann Beier

When he moved to Alliston in the late 1980s, Hermann came into his own as an avid entrepreneur. In this local strip mall, he established a budgie store and planned to open his own pool and darts establishment. Further down the row was his martial arts/health and fitness centre.

But visibility — *profile* — was Hermann's cherished and desperately sought-after goal. He increasingly linked his self-esteem to his businesses. They were a direct reflection of his values.

As if renovations and Hapkido weren't enough, Hermann soon took on another business: "Somebody come to me one day and offered me a good deal on a weight-loss clinic, at the time called Hollywood Weight Loss Clinic, and I paid five thousand dollars [for the] franchise and took it into my fitness centre."

The big-time name of the franchise led to a desire to really push the envelope. But Hermann realized that he needed more space. "So I found a place in town. This lady offers me [another] franchise ... the Beverly Hills Weight Loss Clinic. I opened the business in 1991. Spent a couple of thousand dollars on the franchise and opened it up. It began very well."

With the Beverly Hills weight-loss franchise providing a steady income, Hermann was solidly entrenched as a small-town entrepreneur, with his three-unit section in the Dufferin Street South plaza. He had opened a bird specialty store, Harlequin Place, in one unit; the fitness centre was next door; and Hermann had plans to open a billiard hall in the third unit — the space had been rented and a sign was made and hung over the entrance. Despite the economic downturn, Hermann also continued to operate his renovation business.

He was big on advertising. He had an advertisement that ran with the banner "Harlequin Place" across the top and was decorated with drawings of a budgie and a sheepdog:

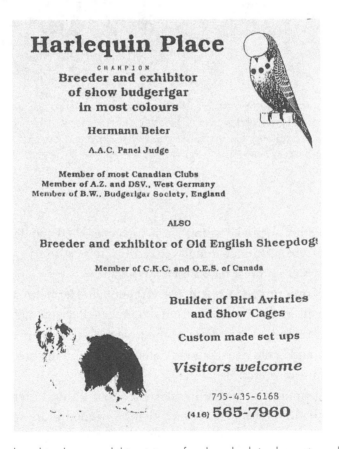

Harlequin Place

CHAMPION
**Breeder and exhibitor
of show budgerigar
in most colours**

Hermann Beier

A.A.C. Panel Judge

**Member of most Canadian Clubs
Member of A.Z. and DSV., West Germany
Member of B.W., Budgerigar Society, England**

ALSO

Breeder and exhibitor of Old English Sheepdogs

Member of C.K.C. and O.E.S. of Canada

**Builder of Bird Aviaries
and Show Cages**

Custom made set ups

Visitors welcome

705-435-6168
(416) **565-7960**

Hermann loved to draw, and this picture of a show budgie decorates a local ad for his Harlequin Place shop, where he also promoted his contractor skills and his dog breeding. He was popular enough that he ran for local councillor just before the robberies; even in prison, he still garnered more than a hundred votes.

For his handyman business, Hermann ran the following advertisement:

Hermann was known for being pretty handy with his tools. He worked to build a strong clientele at his handyman business, but after the recession of the early 1990s, business fell off. This advertisement was used in flyers and in the local newspaper.

The fitness centre was also well advertised:

Hermann became a popular person in the Alliston community, placing extensive ads for his health and fitness centre in the local papers. This ad appeared in a local flyer.

Things were moving along, but his frustrating love life continued to interrupt the continuity, confusing Hermann. A question that kept popping up in his mind was, how can I love these Canadian women? He felt they had a different value system than him.

"All the frustrations that happened to me, especially in the last three years, especially losing girlfriends — because I always get told I'm a very gentle person to women, they love me, enjoy to be with me, but after a while ex-girlfriends told me 'Hermann you're a wonderful man, but I cannot handle you.' This means for them I'm too gentle, you know? Open doors, putting on their coats…. Open the door of the car. For me, Canadian women [should] want this kind of service from the boyfriend, husband, but if they have this kind of person like this, somehow they are shocked. I never cheat on a woman. I never use bad language. I never swear.

"I'm a very muscular person and in the same moment I'm a very gentle person inside. I have a very soft heart and I'm very … I'm looking for that word … candlelight … *Romantic!* This has happened that the woman or ex-girlfriend always love[s] to be with me, but in the end I don't know why, I cannot tell you, [then they're] gone!" He snapped his fingers. "Two women told me 'Hermann, we can be friends, but I cannot handle you.'"

He paused at this point and stared at the walls of the prison common room. Down the hallway, we could hear people talking. Harsh whispers were unintelligible, and maddeningly so, distorted from caroming off the walls.

He continued. "Finally, in 1991, I met this woman [Lana, who] I knew already in the 80s, but she had a boyfriend and I had a girlfriend at the time."

Lana became the love of his life, and his fiancée. "We were going to get married on December 28, 1991. This is the one. I still love her. I hurt her and she left me. I hurt her and I feel sorry for this. Sometimes I'm still sitting and crying [over her]."

(Lana stuck by Hermann's side during his trial and even planned to marry him in prison, but Hermann said she ended up abandoning him and selling most of his possessions, releasing only a few items to his sister Helga in April 1993. When I attempted to contact her in

1993, she refused to speak to me over the phone, if only to counter Hermann's comments, and threatened to call her lawyer if she was bothered again.)

In an April 1993 letter, Hermann wrote about Lana and his other former girlfriends: "Everyone was, more or less, only [wanting] me for good sex and [for the fact that] I am a businessman with money. Especially my last one, my fiancée Lana, who promised me, after my arrest, to stay with me, love me forever, and still want to get married; but in the moment the money was gone what I gave her, also all monies used from items she sold from my businesses, far under-priced, she left me and took off with someone else. In the end she sold more items, including my Caddy [Cadillac] without my knowledge. She moved ... around, changed her phone [numbers], too, [so that] I don't ... write or phone her anymore. We were fighting for a long time in the DC [detention centre, where he was awaiting trial] for the permit to get married. Now I believe this fight was only from one side, only from me."

It degenerated to the point, Hermann said, that when he was at the detention centre during his trial, he had to ask Lana for "canteen money" to buy snack foods. She provided this for a while, apparently, but then stopped, and then Hermann had to resort to asking friends and relatives for money.

Hermann suddenly straightened up and shifted the conversation away from Lana and the other women in his life. He spoke of his vision of himself as a leader, a supporter of other people's dreams and aspirations. This vision was based on the idea of having power and control over one's life. "All my life I always fixed my own problems. I never asked someone. If I would ask as a young person, nobody would help me, but as a person I always helped people. As a young teenager already I helped people, always. Like a psychiatrist."

But the time came when Hermann felt that the control he had worked so hard for was slipping away. The money he was making — and there was a great deal of it at various times — was disappearing into a sinkhole just to keep the businesses afloat. At stake was his livelihood, yes, but also his prestige, his position in the community. The mayor and the good citizens of Alliston had come to see him as a successful member of the community.

"Somehow inside me I was frustrated ... [trying] to keep my business going. I had some money, but not enough."

He claimed to have lost $50,000 or more on his businesses. And he was manipulated by others, he told me: "Screwing up from other people, screwing up from ex-workers."

But Joanne saw it differently. "He took on projects that were too big for him," she said. "He would put a sunroom on a house that was one hundred years old and it would develop leaks. He built a side entrance to a basement and he didn't quite know what he was doing."

In 1990, Hermann went to a small business office of a federal government agency in Barrie to seek help to keep the handyman business going. As Hermann told it, "This young fellow, he said, 'Hermann, it's no problem.'" The office sent several young people to Hermann for training as part of an apprenticeship program.

But the banks were a disappointment, and when I interviewed Hermann he was still bitter about his experiences with them. He was angry with the Canadian banking system because of an advertisement he had seen that claimed people could borrow money with great ease. He saw the banks as great teasers, putting out the illusion of having money for the asking, and then, when the asking was done, of not following through on their promise.

He explained: "So, I get from a few banks, 'Oh, you are a good [credit risk]. Come to us [and we'll] give you so much money.' I phone or call them and they say 'But sir you need something [collateral].' I say I don't have anything. 'Then we cannot give you money.' Why do they call in the first place if I don't have collateral? I went to the federal bank and asked for a credit between $50,000 and $70,000. They said it was peanuts to them, pocket money, and I said great, give me the pocket money. Two weeks later I get denied. I asked why. [They said,] 'Again, you have nothing [to give] and now starts the recession.' I want to help people become what Canadian people need, apprenticeship, skill, trades. Now I get screwed because I can teach, and now boom!"

Hermann seethes when he thinks back to the situation, remembering how the frustration and resentment snaked their way inside him, curling up and spitting venom. That frustration, soon to turn to desperation, metamorphosed in various ways, setting deep roots and affecting the way he conducted his personal relationships. Hermann may have been close to losing his businesses, but he still had himself — proud, strong, and capable.

He admitted that *just maybe* he was a little too cocky, for instance around the local police.

"You see the police sitting in the doughnut shop ... I make jokes [about] this because I'm fifty and I have a good body. I'm a show-off like bodybuilders, but I feel as a fifty-year-old man I have a body that, when I go to the doctor, I get told I'm like thirty-five years old. And I'm proud of this. I'm not a show-off person, but.... " He pauses. "If I talk to my friends in Alliston police [force], for instance, I say 'guys, come to my fitness centre.' He [a police officer] looks like doughnuts [Hermann makes motions to imitate rippling of body fat under his shirt], especially in the summer when they wear their uniform with all the guns and sticks. How can you chase someone? You run one block and you're finished. The criminal laughs at you. And they say 'Hermann, you're right.' Same thing, I went to the OPP and they say 'Hermann, you're right.'"

That led to an idea. Maybe he could drum up some business at the local police stations. Perhaps he could turn the negative relationship into a positive one.

"I went to a few OPP stations. I was in Bradford, I was in Caledon East, I was in Woodbridge, I was in Barrie, and in Alliston. I said 'Come on in guys, learn self-defence or at least work out. I can help you.' Nothing. Excuses." According to Hermann, they told him they were walking their entire shifts, and when they got home, they were tired all the time. "I see the point," he continued, "but the point for me is if you want something, you can do it. All my life I do it. If I want something, I can do it. It's all up here in my mind. So, that is because of [being] lazy? I don't know. I don't blame anybody, but these guys [sit] steady in the cars, steady in the doughnut place, and I [was] getting frustrated."

So to him the police were lazy and unmotivated and did not fit the image of the strong, upstanding police officer with which Hermann was raised. He began to see other faults in the constabulary, as well, such as discrimination and harassment of various Alliston residents.

Photo by John Cooper

Hermann in Millhaven, 1993. He was considered to be a model inmate who worked to stay out of trouble and focused on ways to spend his time productively.

"[You might] see somebody on the street, like a young fellow who was arrested for drinking or because of whatever, being harassed. I'm not talking drugs, I hate drugs, but why the police still harass these people when they want to show now they want to have a better life or they want to change their life, but they will still get hassled.

"Because if you [are arrested] one time … if you're one time in jail, they are always watching you. And I said: Why? I talked to a few officers in Alliston. I said, 'Why you do this? This is not fair; this man wants to show you now how he changed.' My ex-girlfriend from Alliston, her son [used to] get harassed all the time. I told her, 'This is not right.' She was sometimes crying.

"You have to understand all these frustrations. Here the money, here the police, here you get no help, and somehow, someday, I freaked out." He snapped his fingers.

"Okay. Why I robbed a bank is another story."

But that was the end of the first interview. My time was up, and I was told by a guard it was time to leave. It was at that point that I really noticed the Norval Morisseau-style artwork — buffalo shapes and flowing lines swept across the yellow-brick canvas of the back wall of the room, a splash of bright colours that interrupted the beige and grey that dominated the space. The edges of the painting seemed to reach tentatively for the window, as if seeking escape. The afternoon sunlight streaming into the room was sliced into neat sections by the louvred steel shutters and made geometric patterns on the wall. Against this backdrop, I took a couple of photographs of Hermann. Gazing steadily into the lens, he gave me a hopeful, tentative half-smile. He looked like a man who was getting used to his new environment, but was uncertain about the future.

4

Millhaven, Visit Number Two

My second visit to Hermann took place a couple of months after the first. This time, I found him unkempt. He needed a shave, and his hair, which was previously neat and orderly, was in disarray. He also seemed agitated and angry.

He swore twice in reference to the conditions in the prison and his treatment by the guards. This would not be out of the ordinary, not given the invectives being tossed about in that under-the-breath conspiratorial tone used by inmates on the work range, but Hermann always maintained that he never swore. But when he did, he spat the word out with anger and frustration. He put every gram of his energy into it, using the words sparingly but effectively to mould the curve of his anger: "Bullshit!" Everything was bullshit.

It turned out that what was really bothering him was his hip, which had been shattered by a police bullet during the chase. He told me it still hurt like hell. He also couldn't exercise the way he used to and he had gained twenty pounds. He couldn't understand why the authorities couldn't get him the operation he needed so that he might return to regular exercise. When I spoke with the lawyers who dealt with Hermann's civil matters, Paula Beard and her husband James Carlisle, they agreed that approval for the operation was taking a long time. A Mississauga specialist had agreed to do the operation, but the wait was starting to wear on Hermann's nerves.

"The more I gain weight, it puts pressure on the hips," he told me, his hands gripping at the air. "Sitting twenty-two hours a day or lying on a bed and doing nothing [but] drawing. I get told in the detention centre that when you go to the penitentiary it will get easy. It's the same bullshit here. People don't realize how much pain I have."

He was ticked off because some people thought he was arrogant, but he explained that the perceived arrogance was because of his military background and martial arts training. He said he carried himself with self-assurance and confidence and many in the prison didn't like it. "I am a comfortable person and this is why I walk straight. Some people feel that I am an arrogant person."

We were sitting in the common room, and Hermann fidgeted on the wooden seat. To one side, a plate window of smoked glass concealed a circular guard room. Inside, personnel could observe our interview area, the hallway leading to it, and another large cafeteria-style room. A shadowy figure could be seen just barely discernible inside, shifting from one position to another.

Hermann admitted that he didn't fit well in the prison culture, although other inmates respected him for his bank robberies and police shootout. Simultaneously, other inmates left him alone.

"I'm not proud of what I did; don't get me wrong, it [the respect] is just how it works. If you are a drug dealer, they help each other, everyone. If you are just an outsider, you get nothing here."

He wanted desperately to get on the work range — to do things with his hands, keep his mind occupied. Each hour spent in his cell, though he focused on drawing and writing letters, was hell for him. (Later, in a letter, he told me about getting onto the work range — a sought-after goal, and of being involved in an anger management course with other inmates, which he felt helped him channel his rage.)

$

During the interview, Hermann told me about his life before he came to Canada.

Hermann was born in East Germany on August 18, 1941. His family moved to West Germany during the Second World War.

Hermann's father had served in the army. Born in 1902, he had left home during the First World War due to a family dispute, signed up, and served for a couple of years. It was during this time that he came to love wearing a uniform, loved its orderliness and sense of unquestioned purpose, and passed that love on to Hermann.

During his working life, Hermann's father was employed as a warden in a penitentiary. There was not much contact between father and son. "My father was there, but he went early in the morning to work and came back late at night. His [home] life was just to have dinner, read the newspaper, and watch TV. He would iron his shirts and pants, because he wanted to have it this way [neat], and then he went to bed. Unlike other father-son relationships, where father and son did things together, I had nothing."

But then Hermann pulled back and asserted that this lack of paternal attention was a positive, because it made him independent and self-sufficient: "In one way I am proud of this.... I can do anything for my house, because I [had] two sisters and I learned how to handle a house and I like to do it. I can do shopping, cleaning, sewing ..."

And his father told him he was proud to have a son "because his name would carry on."

At seventeen, Hermann entered the military for mandatory service, and then applied to go in for a long stretch, looking at it as a possible career. In the service he learned to shoot, learned to handle radio transmissions, and was often on special assignment duty for his captain.

A can of spoiled fish ruined his plans. After six weeks in the hospital, he returned to his unit, but something had changed. Perhaps the original zest for military service was gone. He was discharged after eighteen months with the rank of corporal. Two years later, while on reserve duty, he earned the rank of sergeant.

After his time in the military, and at his father's urging, Hermann applied to the police department. But at about five foot seven (168 centimetres), he was two centimetres too short for the German police at the time. So it seemed that a career as a police officer was out of the question.

Jobs with uniforms were getting scarce. His father suggested he come to work at the penitentiary, but Hermann had taken metalworking courses at a trade school and had secured a job at a metal fabrication plant in Hamm, northeast of Dortmund.

He also had found the time to marry (at age seventeen), and he and his wife already had four children. "At the time, I was working in a metal factory, and I was leading a group of people, and I made good money, so I said 'Why do I want to change?'" He had a family to support, and he needed to earn money. His budgie breeding was also taking up an increasing amount of his time.

The lure of a government job, with its security and good pension, was tempting, but Hermann was focused on what he had at the time — it would have been too much of a sacrifice for him to give up his factory job for something new. But despite having a good, steady job, Hermann had still not purged his fascination with uniformed authority and everything it had come to represent. "I tried to come to help the police. I was out with them a few times, like a student to watch them." He explained that this "auxiliary police role" was common in Germany.

His wife Renata, he told me, was a "wonderful woman" who was "always go, go, go. She was totally the opposite [to me] and sometimes I realize that she was not the right person for me, but it never occurred to me [to leave]. I am a one-woman man and I wouldn't leave her because of the children."

In 1968, when Hermann was twenty-seven, the family moved to Heppingserbach, near Hemer, where Hermann worked in construction and at other part-time jobs to support his brood. He later earned good money — up to $1,500 a month — at a full-time job in a wire factory. It was hard and tiring work, and Hermann said he sometimes logged as many as three hundred hours in a month. The dedication paid off, however, when the company made him a supervisor. He was at the job for twelve years, up until the time he came to Canada.

Meanwhile, both of his sisters had immigrated to Canada. After Hermann's mother died in 1971, the decision to move became easier for him, though it would take another nine years for the dream to become a reality.

His mother's death was a riveting experience for Hermann. She had been sick with cancer for three years, racked with pain from the disease and the treatments. Then she had gall bladder problems. The resulting surgery resulted in the removal of a stone half the size of a chicken egg.

Hermann, who was busy with his own home renovations, took time out in November of 1971 to go to his mother's house to help her redecorate. He painted, he papered the walls, he even wallpapered the ceilings, a practice he said was popular with many Germans.

He had just finished papering the hallway ceiling — his mother helping by holding up part of the paper with a broom handle.

"Mom, I am done," he said.

She told him, "Yes, you did a very good job."

She looked around and smiled, then collapsed.

"I didn't know what happened when somebody died. She slid to the floor and I caught her. I went to the neighbour, who had a phone, and called an ambulance. These things take five minutes, but for me it was like half an hour. They arrived and took her to the hospital, but she was [already] dead. I always ask, *Why me? Why she died in my arms?* [There] must be some meaning…. We were very close. After this, that was the only time I came close to my father."

His relationship with his father deepened. "He wanted nobody else around anyway. At the time, my marriage was falling apart. At one time, he said 'Leave Renata, she's not a good wife,' and this and [that] … I said 'Pop, she's still my wife and the children are still small.'"

At Christmas 1973, Hermann's father offered to pay for his son to travel to Canada to visit one of his sisters (Renate). Hermann jumped at the chance and fell in love with the country during his trip. Upon his return to Germany, he immediately applied to emigrate.

Though denied time after time, he persisted: "Every year I would request to make a new application and I always get denied. And finally, [in]1979, I made arrangement at the beginning of the year to come to visit my sister."

This was after a second visit in 1977: "I made the arrangements to come to Canada with my wife and see how it works out." He was hopeful that his wife would love the country as much as he did, and give the green light to emigrating.

That third trip involved a bus tour of North America, which included a stop in Seattle to visit the grave of martial arts legend Bruce Lee. Hermann had been a fan of the charismatic Lee since his oldest son's involvement in martial arts. Hermann used to drop his son off at the martial arts school, but one day he stayed and watched for awhile. He soon became absorbed in the regimen, order, and power of the sport, and began taking lessons himself. (My requests to Hermann for additional information about his instructor and the whereabouts of the school was met with a response that it had closed several years before and that the instructor didn't speak English.) On weekends, he took his son to watch Bruce Lee movies.

The bus trip was a treat for Hermann. "I get the crazy idea when I go to Canada ... I said, I want to visit Seattle, where is Bruce Lee's grave." The bus company offered a two-week round trip for $279, starting in Toronto, then two days each in New York, San Francisco, Seattle, and Vancouver before returning to Toronto.

"I went to the grave of Bruce Lee. It took almost forever to find it because nobody knows where Bruce Lee is." For Hermann, this was unacceptable — a star of Lee's magnitude would make it essential that locals would know where he was buried. His eyes tighten up at the thought. "Anyway, I was standing and paying my respect at the grave for two hours, and then from there we went to Vancouver and on back to Toronto."

Unfortunately, the marriage wouldn't survive the trip. "When we came back from this visit, I took my stuff and left the house," he told me.

The marriage had lasted twenty years. "But she was a wonderful woman. She was a good housewife. She didn't work because I worked my butt off to support the family. I believe today I worked too much. I didn't spend enough time for myself and if not for my family, just for myself."

His marriage over, Hermann went to the Canadian Consul in Bonn and made a personal request for permission to emigrate. Before, there had been excuses — Hermann's poor English, for example — but this time his persistence paid off and he was granted permission to emigrate. He arrived in Canada on May 5, 1980, and at first stayed with his sister Renata. After a couple of months, he moved to Oakville, where he lived for two years.

But there was so much more to tell, and Hermann was just getting warmed up. In the second part of our interview he wanted to talk more about his life and about the crimes he committed, and to provide some sort of rationale for what he did.

5

BACK AGAINST THE WALL

OUTSIDE THE INTERVIEW ROOM, GUARDS AND OFFICIALS WENT ABOUT their duties with practised ease, in an atmosphere of watchful wire-spring tension. Such is the nature of prison life — the inmates are watched, and they watch back. Nobody relaxes "inside," except perhaps when the lights are off and the doors are closed and locked.

But Hermann, focused as he was on his own life, could create a bubble of disinterest and distance from the outside world, and talk with his own brand of enthusiasm about what motivated him. He explained to me why he was so angry with the police, with the banks, and with the circumstances of his own life. Before the robberies, Hermann said he was driven by factors beyond his control, by anger and disgust at the laziness of the police, and by his belief that he could find a chink in their armour and show them up for the inadequate souls he thought them to be. He believed that they could be, should be outwitted, outsmarted, and shown up for being inept.

Simultaneously, he was trying to live up to the expectations of his father, who was by that time long dead, and reach for goals he thought he would never achieve. He had lost money, girlfriends, self-esteem, and, most important perhaps, time — he was getting old.

And the banks, the financial powerhouses that withheld their largesse from him ... well, to take from them would be nothing, no more than skimming cream off the top of the milk.

As we spoke, these notions were woven into the fabric of Hermann's remarks. Like a pattern in a sweater, a line of thought appeared along a sleeve and disappeared into an explanation along the seam, reappeared in a pocket, then disappeared again into a collar, where another idea, another compelling thread, colourful and rich, would take over. He wore his coat of interpretation well. The details — all of them — were all so compelling to Hermann.

Was there an *exact* reason for the commission of his crimes — could they be reduced to one single overriding factor? Probably not. It may have been lost in the labyrinthine twists and turns of his conscience. One thing he was clear on was the feeling that came packaged with every deed: "It's a terrible feeling to go in a bank with a gun in hand, to say to someone, 'Give me the money.'" He says this with a husky voice and clear eyes.

He repeated to me several times that the gun he used in the robberies was not loaded, as if this would excuse the fear he brought to a teller's eyes: "The gun was never loaded. My .22 that I had in my hand, it was never loaded, never equipped, never was [there] a bullet. At the moment I felt that my heart was racing, triple time of the normal speed. I was close more to a heart attack than anything else because [it had] never, never occurred to me to do [this] in all my life. If you watch TV, it's so easy for people, but if you do it yourself it's … a terrible feeling, a terrible feeling. I couldn't sleep for days after.

"And you're not happy to have money in your hand at all. The money I used that I got from these [robberies] was just to pay off my debts. I never had debts in my whole life. I always paid debts my whole life."

The subject of the banks entered his mind. "The reason, this is not nice to say, but I am disappointed that the bank didn't help me. And they make a big paper [advertisements] to offer help for small business people. Then you go over there and ask for help and they say 'No, we can't.' So I say to them, 'So shut up and don't put these papers out.'

"I know it's not nice to say, but you don't hurt anybody if you take the money from the bank. I never could do it from a private home or a jewellery store or whatever. It took me days to go over this point to do it in the bank."

To achieve a state of mind where he could steal, where he could point a gun at someone's head without breaking a sweat, without shaking,

Hermann watched many films about robberies. He consumed anything that focused on bank thefts and violence. He gorged himself on bloodshed and gunfire late into the night.

"I pushed myself, in watching TV and movies, criminal movies, like robberies, like [somebody] takes drugs to push you to this moment. I had to make myself ready to do this."

While he prepared to conduct the robberies, Hermann also downed large quantities of what he described as "Chinese power pills." These were ginseng capsules, readily available in any health food store or pharmacy. Famous for the curative, energy-enhancing properties of its root, ginseng has been popular in Asia for centuries. Historically, the simple herb, a native of temperate Asian woodlands, was so sought-after that wars were fought over control of the forests where it grew wild.

Its popularity had accelerated rapidly over the past three decades; North American farmers were cashing in on ginseng's value, growing fields of it for use in herbal concoctions, from pills and liquids to chewable tablets. In the early 1980s, a top quality root could sell for up to $10,000.

In studies, ginseng has shown a wide range of properties, some of them so astounding as to have earned the root a reputation as a wonder drug. Stephen Fulder, a doctor of pharmacology and author of *The Tao of Medicine*, says ginseng is an effective stimulant, with the ability to improve vitality and increase energy levels and endurance. According to Fulder, it even enhances brain power, with test subjects working faster, more accurately, and committing fewer errors on tasks.

So safe is ginseng that it is hard for pharmacologists to determine a lethal dose. According to Fulder, it would take more than two kilograms of ginseng in one dose to kill an adult male. In experiments on mice, maximum doses caused enlarged stomachs (from overeating), but the subjects were otherwise well.

Dr. Fulder does note some side effects, however: "There may be side effects arising from the over-arousal, which may occur in people who are naturally excited, nervous, and high-strung. The side effects might take the form of irritability, sleeplessness, and raised blood pressure."

Caffeine is not recommended for ginseng users, says Fulder. As a stimulant, caffeine intensifies ginseng's effect.

Hermann felt some effects of excessive ginseng use. Besides staying up late, he suffered from stomach aches. In response, he began taking large quantities of the antacid tablet Rolaids, sometimes up to 140 tablets a day, he said. Rolaids are calcium-based, and Hermann later worried about the effects of excess calcium on his system. His own research led him to believe that excess calcium could cause anger, irritability, and psychosis.

Psychosis is a very broad term and was rarely used by psychiatrists in describing mental disorders, according to Henry Gleitman in his book *Psychology*. Psychosis covers a wide range of problems, mainly associated with a reduced ability to differentiate between fantasy and reality: "In psychoses, the patient's thoughts and deeds no longer meet the demands of reality."

Later, Hermann's lawyer, Paul Stern, told me in a telephone conversation that he researched this "calcium connection" while preparing Hermann's defence, but that he could find no evidence of it anywhere. I later spoke with my family doctor, who consulted her husband, also a physician and a specialist in internal medicine. Neither had found evidence of any studies showing a connection between excessive calcium intake and psychosis.

Can a state of psychosis be induced by calcium? It just doesn't happen, the experts say.

Hermann said he was not a drug abuser or a heavy drinker, and he didn't use any drugs or alcohol to put him in an altered state of mind to commit his crimes. His sole motivation, other than the vague but possible sense of power and invincibility (combined with sleeplessness) induced by the ginseng, came from watching movies.

Hermann started watching violent movies, perhaps even becoming addicted to them. He claimed that the overabundance of violence on television and in the movies — whether videos or television shows — created in him a tolerance to violence, and that the influence of the media pushed him to be a more violent person, to accept that taking risks would be okay, and that the suspension of reality that came with violent films could easily be transferred to real life. He said it was "like drugs or drinking alcohol. You drink, drink, drink, drink until you're drunk. And this is [the same with] the movies ... because this introduces people [to the idea of doing] some violence. I found it in my own body now, my own experience; [I believed] you can do it if you want to. I feel like — it's not an excuse; don't get me wrong, it's not an excuse — I felt that I was pushed in this direction."

I thought for a moment of Hermann's reference to — and reverence for — Bruce Lee, and it reminded me of a scene from the movie *Dragon: The Bruce Lee Story*, where Bruce Lee, played by Jason Scott Lee, is travelling on a boat from China to the United States. He sits next to a fellow passenger, also Chinese, and asks if he speaks English. The man nods. "I want to practise my English," Lee says with a smile, then goes on to speak of the great opportunities of America. The word drips with gold and honey: *America*. I wonder whether it wasn't perhaps this vision of perfection that Hermann also had in mind when he came to this continent — the clichéd and imperfect vision of streets paved with gold — and why, when everything went so wrong and his dreams derailed, he fell so hard.

Hermann idly rubbed his hands on his jeans. He looked as if he was deep in thought. When he finally continued, he again spoke about his reasons for committing the crimes. Hermann seemed to grope around blindly, trying to find the words to describe the tapestry of raw feelings that motivated him. He began rationalizing, justifying, and burying guilt and remorse, lending some small measure of explanatory credence to his violent acts.

His father, the prison superintendent, was a strict man, a man with expectations, he said. And Hermann wanted to follow in his footsteps. He spoke again of the desire to be a man in uniform, a man of authority. "I wanted to be … a policeman. In 1983 or 1984, I applied to become a policeman. That is why [it's] so disappointing for me. First of all, I understand that you have to be a Canadian citizen. I became, in the beginning of 1984, a Canadian citizen. Not for only becoming a policeman, but also because I love Canada …

"So, I became a Canadian citizen and I applied again to become a policeman. Then I hear all of a sudden I'm too old. I said 'I was just here last year and nobody told me this.' I know a lot of police officers; they [were] my friends at the time. They say 'Hermann, if you still want to be a policeman, go to the airport police.'"

While his English was passable, the airport, representing both official languages, also demanded facility in French. "I filled out the application and everything was fine until it come to language. You have to have a second language. That is great because I speak German. 'No, no, no, you have to have French' [they told me]. I said 'What kind of bullshit is that?' Why French? It's not just French people in the airport. It's going to be Italian, German, you name it, and it's nice that all of a sudden somebody speaks German in the airport when somebody has a problem. [They said] 'No, no, French.' So, I was disappointed and never tried again, because you get older not younger. That was another disappointment."

I believed that the series of events that led to the robberies was mitigated somewhat by his jack of all trades attitude to life — the budgie breeding and dog raising, the handyman business, the bird sanctuary, the various women in his life. I wondered, though, whether he was already headed for trouble, even in the mid-1980s, when his life still looked pretty good. Soon I would find out just how rough life could get, when Hermann, and others, would tell the story of the bank robberies he committed, in minute-by-minute play-by-play. An event like that is something you remember, and Hermann would have the rest of his life to wrestle with the details.

6

Halloween 1991

Nineteen ninety-one was a banner year for robberies: 1,611 were committed, compared to 1,530 the following year. According to *Canadian Banker*, the average take was $1,500; 47 percent of holdups resulted in less than $1,000 being stolen. Two-thirds of the holdups occurred in seven major cities across Canada.

Seventy-eight percent of robberies are committed by lone individuals. Sixty-seven percent used no disguise, 40 percent had a holdup note, and in 45 percent of the robberies bank staff detected no weapons. Bank employees were injured in ten of the offences. The traditional payday, Thursday, was the most popular day for holdups (365), followed by Friday (360). April 25 and October 31, 1991, were both Thursdays.

According to the 1993 Metro Police Annual Report, holdups of financial institutions had increased by 31 percent (the Greater Toronto Area accounts for up to one-quarter of the national tally). Two out of three robberies involved guns or other weapons; handguns showed a 30 percent jump in use over the previous year. To compensate, police officials received increased pressure to increase holdup squad staff numbers.

On October 30, 1991, Hermann Beier set into motion the two-day whirlwind of events that would lead to his eventual arrest. At 5:45 a.m., and calling himself "Mr. Bruce" (in tribute perhaps, to Bruce Lee? Though I never asked), Hermann contacted a limousine company, asking to be picked up at the Skyline Hotel near Pearson International Airport. When limousine driver Nasib Singh Mander pulled into the driveway of the Skyline, he had no idea that a routine fare would turn into a ride of terror.

After getting into the car, Hermann pointed his gun at Mander's head and ordered him to drive north on Highway 27. Mander could feel the cold steel of the gun barrel pressing into the flesh of his neck.

Mander, who gave his court testimony with the assistance of a Punjabi-speaking interpreter, told the court Hermann said to him, "Don't try to jump out or I'll shoot you and kill you." The words were deliberate, calm, and unfeeling.

Given his instruction, Mander drove north on Highway 27, then took a side road to Highway 50. During the ride, he was ordered to keep to the speed limit to avoid drawing police attention.

Hermann asked about the quantity of fuel in the propane-powered car, as he had plans to travel to Kingston. Those plans quickly changed. On a side road off Highway 50, Mander was told to pull over. Hermann then ordered him to put his money on the dashboard and get out of the car. It was a desolate area, a county side road with only a few houses dotting the landscape.

Mander figured this was the end of his life. As he told the court: "It appeared to be the last minute of my life and I was thinking it's very easy for him to kill me because there was nobody around, nobody was passing either way and there were trees and it was isolated place like a jungle. It was the right place for him to kill me. I was very scared."

Mander walked away from the car, picking up speed, but, though tempted, he didn't dare break into a run; he turned and saw Hermann get into the driver's seat and speed off. At a nearby home, Mander received assistance from a man who called police from the cellular phone in his van.

More than a year and a half later, Mander told me over the phone that he still had nightmares about the incident. While he had an interpreter in court, his English was very good. He agreed to speak to me the next day at his home.

His apartment was in a less-than-stellar high rise in North York's Finch Avenue/Dufferin Street area. The hallways were, to put it frankly, not pristine, and it had the look of a place where a less-than-welcoming Canada puts its new citizens, but where people with dreams of a better life might get their start.

I knocked on an apartment door several times. Finally, a woman wearing a sari answered. As the door swept open, a co-mingling scent of flowers and spice opened a tiny but meaningful crack in the stale odour of the hallway.

"There is no Nasib Singh Mander here," she told me. Her English was quiet, firm and precise. I was surprised. I double checked the address. I knocked on a few more doors. It was an apartment building largely peopled with new Canadians; they were distrustful of me, their eyes downcast or glazed over in a way that made it clear there was no information forthcoming. "Stay away from us, we don't trust you," their eyes said to me, and could I really blame them?

I left the building. *Why wasn't he up front with me?* I asked myself. *Why did he say he would meet when he obviously didn't intend to?*

Outside, a stiff sheet of sleet stung my face; my eyes were smarting. I called Mander's number from the pay phone of a hamburger place across the street. A woman answered. "He is not here," she told me. Her English was clipped and precise.

"We had an appointment," I said. "I came up to his apartment." I gave her the address and apartment number. "I may have spoken to you. If I did, why didn't you tell me then that he was not at home?"

"He is not here," she said, emotionless, and hung up. I tried to rationalize. Perhaps Mr. Mander didn't believe in the entrenched rights and freedoms of our society. He was free; Hermann Beier was in prison. Why couldn't he see that?

Maybe there was fear, a concern that his life was not much different from that of the cabbies who risked their necks in downtown Toronto every night. And it only took one morning in October for Mander to find that out.

At about 9:50 on the morning of October 30, Hermann (he says he was forced to plead guilty to the charges stemming from this incident; regardless, the court records were very clear on what happened) entered the Canadian Imperial Bank of Commerce in Brechin. If you drive north on Highway 12, east of Lake Simcoe, you might still see the bank, just the sort of square, sturdy building where the locals in a rural community would keep their cash. The four corners of the small downtown area (now part of the Township of Ramara) is the kind of proverbial place that you might miss if you blink as you pass through on the way to Orillia.

The bank robber that morning was dressed completely in black, with long black hair that flowed down onto his shoulders. A black bandanna was pulled over his face up to his nose. He entered the bank, then walked up to teller Beth McCarthy and pulled out a handgun and a plastic bag. He ordered her to put money in the bag. While McCarthy filled it, the thief pointed toward the main vault and said he wanted money from there. He also asked for money from adjacent teller Debbie Farrell's drawer.

He went to the bank manager's office, pointed the gun at her, and waved a smoke bomb (which resembled a hand grenade) around as he repeated his demand for money from the vault. Told that the vault was on a timer system, he instead demanded money from the tellers' timer boxes, which were on ten-minute timers. He gave up on that, noticed another teller, and got money from her drawer instead. He left the bank with $10,690.

Within forty minutes, he struck again, this time at the CIBC branch in Woodville, a small community of a few hundred in the Kawartha region of central Ontario, west of Lindsay. At 10:30 he entered the branch and instructed an elderly customer to step back from the counter. With the gun in one hand and a plastic shopping bag in the other, he approached the only teller, a Ms. Jordan-Otter. He pointed the gun at her and demanded money. A total of $5,664 was placed in the bag. Again, he wanted money from the vault, but the timer system prevented access.

The next day, October 31, at 9:05 a.m., Hermann drove to the Royal Bank in Georgetown, a small village-cum-town that at the time had about half of its current population of 40,000; a bit of a bedroom community, it is located sixty kilometres west of Toronto and just west of Brampton, and is nestled snugly in the Halton Hills.

Hermann left the stolen Lincoln in the parking lot and entered the bank wearing a long black wig, false moustache, dark sunglasses, and makeup. He tossed a plastic grocery bag at bank manager Philip Campbell, who was manning one of the wickets, and told him to fill it up. Campbell hesitated and Hermann raised his revolver and pointed it at him. Campbell's till was empty. Hermann had a smoke bomb in his hand. He put his hands together and made a motion suggesting that he would pull the pin out of the cylinder. That got a response, with Campbell and a teller taking money from the top cash drawer at the wicket and filling the bag. Hermann took a look in the bag; unsatisfied, he handed the bag back and motioned to the middle drawer, which was laden with cash. The bag was filled, to a total of $13,876. Satisfied with his haul, Hermann pulled the pin out of the smoke bomb, tossed it into the main customer area, then left the branch as white smoke billowed out.

He got back in the Lincoln and set off toward Rockwood, about a half-hour drive west.

7

Rockwood: "I Won't Hurt the Kids"

Frances Binning was the customer service manager of the Royal Bank on Main Street in Rockwood, and was on duty the day Hermann robbed it. She had been with the bank for twenty-six years.

At that time, the Royal Bank was the only bank in Rockwood, a community of several thousand residents just a fifteen-minute drive northeast of Guelph. It was a busy day, and about nine customers were in the branch that morning.

Staff had been alerted to the fact that a robbery had been committed at the Royal Bank in nearby Georgetown a short time earlier. They weren't necessarily expecting a robbery, but the alert gave them time to prepare. Cash quantities in the tills had been adjusted so that they contained only a minimum amount; bundles of "bait money" (their serial numbers recorded so the money could be traced) had been placed in the drawers.

After an easy drive from Georgetown, Hermann parked the car and entered the bank, still dressed in black: black coat, black sunglasses, and black gloves. "Everything was black," Mrs. Binning told the court. She testified that he wore a wig and a long false moustache, also black.

Hermann was calm, saying few words. He pulled out a gun, came around the counter to Mrs. Binning's desk, and handed her a plastic grocery bag. He told her to fill it. Mrs. Binning went to the cash drawer, opened it, and put the money, including the bait money, into the bag.

The court was told that Hermann seem to become agitated when he saw a frightened teller who had frozen on the spot in the open vault. When he saw this, he had yelled something unintelligible. (Or maybe it was the prospect of more money, the open vault an alluring sight.)

He took the bag back and gave it to teller Carole Rogers, with instructions to place more cash inside. Rogers remembered him as "very calm," and that he spoke with an accent, although she could not tell exactly what kind of accent he had.

Later, during an interview in the summer of 1993, Frances Binning remembered it well. She told me her story calmly, seated in the kitchen of her comfortable home in Fergus, a twenty-five-minute drive from her workplace in Rockwood. There, this mother of two grown children seemed relaxed, placed by time and distance from an event she would remember for the rest of her life. Her husband, Paul, wandered in from the backyard, a compact, smiling man, bare-chested and equally relaxed.

Frances looked the part of the small-town bank manager, with permed hair and glasses, a composed, still-unlined face, and a wry "how could this happen to me?" grin.

Yes, how could it?

She proffered a glass of Coke with ice and eased into a kitchen chair. A black cat purred contentedly, rubbing its arched back against a table leg. On that sunny summer afternoon the memories came floating back.

"We were alerted that the bank in Georgetown was robbed. We were really cautious. My desk sits kitty-corner to the door and I [saw] this figure come in. He just pulled the gun out and I stood up. It seems like you're not really there. It's hard to explain, it's just the fear and everyone is terrified. In the bank there were a lot of people all together [nine], including kids. All the training they give you about a robbery, it all clicks into your head."

Frances headed for a wicket, depositing money, and the marked bait money that bank employees are trained to add, into Hermann's bag. She was calm on the outside, "but there is a feeling that you're in a dream somehow, that it's not happening to you. It's something you never want to have happening to you. When somebody points a gun at you, you don't know if he's going to shoot you."

Royal Bank of Canada, Rockwood, Ontario. Alerted to an earlier robbery, bank employees had time to prepare bait money and reduce the cash in their tills in anticipation of Hermann Beier's arrival. But that didn't prepare them for the two minutes of terror during the robbery.

Frances held the hand of one young woman who began getting upset. Another teller froze. "I yelled at her to snap out of it. You don't want to antagonize him. You don't want him to be violent. You're also staring at him constantly because you think *I've got to describe him*. So you're look-ing at his build, what he's wearing, his gun, his disguise. You couldn't see anything of his [face] except right here [she points to her cheeks]. He had hair way down over his face. You couldn't describe his facial features."

Hermann was neither too nervous nor too aggressive. "He didn't yell or anything when he asked for the money, except when Barb froze [by the vault] … when she froze there, he yelled, but he wasn't hostile. We knew by then he wasn't a druggie. Usually druggies are the ones who rob banks.

"It seemed like an hour, but it was only a couple of minutes," added Frances.

One employee was busy writing down Hermann's description while the robbery was taking place. Another employee, seated in the lunchroom and with a full view of the street, took down the licence number of the Lincoln parked outside.

Hermann took the bag, which contained $35,869, and left. On the way out he said to a customer holding her two small children, "I won't hurt the kids." Despite his disguise, his thick accent was a clue to his identity.

I later contacted Royal Bank headquarters. John Emerson, manager of human resource services for the Royal Bank's Ontario District, informed me that the bank had had an Employee Assistance Program (EAP) in place for more than ten years at the time of the robberies. While post-robbery trauma is not the sole reason for the EAP's existence, the program is especially useful in those cases.

"The program has really proven to be quite beneficial to staff who have been through some kind of trauma," said Emerson. "Representatives of the assistance program go and talk to the staff, to draw out of them the feelings they have in response to the robbery."

Administered by external consultants, the EAP also provides such services as alcohol and marital counselling, with access through a 1-800 number. The aim is to keep people on the job, no matter the source of stress.

"Most of the people go through the program with the intent of staying on the job. The return rate is close to 100 percent. Most of our branches affected by robberies either reopen the same day or are open the next day. I would say just about all the staff report back to work the next day."

With an increase in bank robberies, a program was essential. "Most of our robberies, thank God, are non-violent. They may come in with a gun [or] they may just threaten to have a gun, but you won't see it. But most of the time they just grab the money and run. There is always the possibility that robberies will happen. One of the things that we stress to our staff is 'Don't be a hero.'"

The bank also used a video entitled "It Could Happen to You" to prepare staff in case of a robbery. While one bank robbery may shake you up, a repeat is bound to have an effect on a bank staffer's confidence and sense of security, Emerson said.

It only takes one robbery to make staff members uncertain, and to compel them to act in a more guarded way in the future. "I think in a place like that, in Rockwood or anywhere, the first time, [especially] if

Photo by John Cooper

Increases in bank security, more heavily armed police forces, and significant advances in sophisticated forensic techniques and tracking of criminals make modern banks, like this branch of the Royal Bank in Whitby, Ontario, much more difficult to rob. Many criminals have switched from the very dangerous practice of robbing banks in person to using the Internet to steal funds.

nothing really happened [before] … that has an impact on you." A lack of previous criminal activity would mean that "eventually you get the feeling that you are safe. But if [a robbery] is happening to you repeatedly, your sense of being safe is impacted."

8

Guelph: The Chase Is On

Hermann's next stop was Guelph. At the Royal Bank on York Road, staff was prepared, also having been informed of the earlier Georgetown robbery.

Michelle Poirier was the officer in charge of the branch, which was busy, as were the other branches, because of Canada Savings Bonds coming due November 1. Like the branch in Rockwood, Poirier had ensured that the cash drawers had their robbery-ready minimum, including bait money.

When Hermann arrived, he came around the counter, same long black hair, black coat and pants, and black gloves. The only difference between his appearance here and at Rockwood was the addition of a peaked chauffeur-style cap.

He asked for money. "'Lots of it,'" said Poirier. He stood in front of the cash-dispensing unit, a centralized, one-teller-operated kiosk that served as the sole cash conduit in the bank. Poirier dropped the cash she was holding. It took her a couple of times to get the attention of a teller. Nobody moved. The robber freely pointed his gun, she said, the threat being so palpable that she found it hard to respond when it was clear he wanted her to take the few steps toward him, take the bag, fill it with money from the cash drawer, and hand it back.

Then she and the robber went on a little drawer-by-drawer search. She got some U.S. money from the back. He backed up and moved around the counter. Poirier moved in concert with him, slowly, while he backed out of the bank, continuing to point the gun at the people inside the bank; Poirier was keeping pace with him in order to get a view of his licence plate. As the vehicle left, she yelled out the plate number.

The robbery lasted five minutes, from 10:15 to 10:20 a.m. The total take was $3,798.

Within minutes of the alarm being sounded at the bank, Guelph Police Service Constable Wayne Hummel spotted the suspect at the intersection of Neeve and Wellington Streets. By this time, Hermann had already managed to switch the plates on the car, from New Brunswick to Quebec. Regardless of the plate switch, Hummel knew by the description of the vehicle that he had Hermann in his sights, and began following him as he drove along Wellington.

At a major intersection, Constable Randy Dedman, also of the Guelph Police Service, pulled his cruiser in front of the Lincoln in an attempt to block Hermann's progress. But Hermann turned right onto Gordon Street and then west on Fountain Street.

"I wouldn't stop. I wouldn't stop," Hermann told me, sucking in his breath. "I wouldn't stop."

At another intersection, Hermann jammed the brakes on. Hummel pulled up along the passenger side of Hermann's car, but when he saw the window come down and a gun levelled at him, he hit the accelerator and nosedived forward, a bullet from Hermann's gun shattering the driver's rear side window. (This was in contrast to Hermann's version of events. Hermann claimed the officer pulled a gun on him first.)

"At the same moment he pulled a gun," Hermann told me in our interview. "After this, I would not stop again; *he* pulled the gun. I don't know exactly what happened because everything went ... so fast. Sometimes I still have clips [in my head], sometimes like a picture through milk glasses," which I took to mean foggy or obscured. "All of a sudden he pulled a gun and the gun [went] off."

Again, this contrasted with the officer's recollection of events as told to the court. Hermann continued: "I don't know where he shot me.... I don't know if it hit the car or what. I was so pissed off — I'm sorry, my language — I was so mad. I said, *You son of a gunski! You shoot at me just because* ... it's just the reflex, self-defence. I had one of my guns lying beside me. Just to show him that I had a gun, too, and believe it or not, I know what happened: Pomp! The gun went off. If I pulled the trigger, [it was] an accident."

Hermann then hit the gas and took off down Dublin Street and, after colliding with Dedman's car, continued, with both Hummell and Dedman in pursuit.

"I was not thinking in this moment because my mind was not [registering] that it was a policeman or whatever. The reaction [was] self-defence. I know it's stupid, I know it's not right, but seconds, you know, you make [decisions] sometimes in seconds and then it's too late whatever you do. So, I show my gun, the gun went off, and that's how everything started. I know people would say 'Why you don't stop there?'"

Hermann had a police radio in the Lincoln and could hear the back-and-forth chatter of the police. The pursuit became a dangerous cat-and-mouse game in the normally quiet streets of Guelph. "I put my pedal down and I'm off. Then, all of a sudden, [on] his radio he called up and in a few minutes later [they] chase me with four or five cruisers. At first I was lost. I don't know where … I don't know Guelph at all. I was working in Guelph [once], but in a different direction … not in this part where I was. At the time, after the first shot, it was like my whole body was numb. It was just a funny feeling, if I can use the [word] *funny*, it's not funny, but it is a funny or strange feeling in your body. You're there, but somehow you are dead. You're not there at all. I was feeling like … it was like a suicide. I don't give a damn any more. Just kill me or put me away."

He continued: "Everything runs like a movie, your life. The whole chase, as far as I can remember, the whole thing, is strange. Everything passes by, your life. What you did good, what you did wrong in your life. The whole life passes by in a few minutes. Pictures come back … pictures from Germany. Sometimes [of] your screaming children, sometimes [of] your happy children. You get married. All these funny, strange pictures coming in this second in your mind, but the whole body feels numb."

Shots from Hermann's gun peppered the police vehicles, dangerously close to hitting the officers, but thankfully no one was hit. Hummell instructed bystanders who had come out of their houses for a look to get back inside. Joining the pursuit were Staff Sergeant Near and Sergeant Zinger of the Guelph Police Service. They had observed the shooting at Nottingham and Dublin Streets and had pulled in immediately behind Hermann as he drove up Bristol Street.

At another intersection, Hermann jumped from the Lincoln, turned, and fired several shots. He then got back in the car and continued along Bristol. He tossed a smoke bomb out of the car after he turned up a side street and onto Waterloo Avenue.

In and out of traffic, along the major arterial road, Wellington Street, adjacent to the Speed River, and then onto the Hanlon Expressway, through heavy traffic, Hermann led police on an erratic chase, hitting speeds of 150 to 160 kilometres per hour, sometimes crossing lawns and running whatever red lights there were, passing elementary schools and pedestrians at breakneck speed. At a T-intersection at Delaware Drive, Hermann slammed to a halt again, leaping from the vehicle and shooting at his pursuers. Sergeant Wayde Meyer of the Guelph OPP was the lead vehicle at the time and had to dodge behind his car to avoid the bullets. Hermann got back in the car and the chase continued out of the city along Victoria Road.

With cruisers from the Guelph Police Service and the OPP in pursuit, Hermann got onto Highway 6, throwing more smoke bombs as he turned north onto the Nickel Eramosa Town Line. A low hill lay ahead and Hermann stopped. He took a position of defiance, facing the oncoming officers directly and firing at the police, who pulled up about seventy-five metres away. A flurry of shots hit the police vehicles, some skidding off the hood of one police vehicle and taking out its roof light, before Hermann got back in the car and the pursuit continued.

Hermann made his way through Fergus, then northeast toward Bellwood and south on concession roads 3 and 4. He went east again on County Road 22 and emerged at Brucedale, turning east onto Highway 24. Then it was onto County Road 50 to the 5th line of Erin Township and south to the Erin/Halton Town Line. There, Detective Constable Liz O'Donnell, who would later lead the investigation following Hermann's arrest, and partner Sergeant Dorie of the OPP's Caledon detachment had set up a partial roadblock. Hermann came roaring through it, his left arm out of the window, firing off shots as he sped by.

Around this time, Constable Al Stennett of Halton Regional Police got involved. At the time a nine-year member of the force, he was a family man with a wife, three kids, and a life outside the force — a very good life. When he got the call, he knew something serious was happening, something unprecedented.

Stennett picked up a call during his routine patrol of Georgetown and nearby Acton: an armed robbery was in progress in Georgetown. Earlier, they had received information regarding the stolen Lincoln. Time had elapsed and Hermann had already made his way from Georgetown to Rockwood to Guelph, and was now heading east.

Armed robbery calls had been received before, and even though they were on the increase, they were still quite rare, averaging only about six or seven a year, Constable Stennett told me in the summer of 1993 when I met with him at police headquarters. As he stretched out his six-foot frame, crossing one black boot over the other in the neat confines of a meeting room at the Georgetown detachment, he recounted his experience that day. He looked confident in his full shift uniform, the addition of a neat moustache perhaps making him look older and more authoritative. He was careful to ensure that the details he gave me were accurate and as he had presented them in court.

He remembered gearing himself up mentally for a robbery pursuit. "A lot of calls [over the police radio] unfortunately are pumped up more than they are. You get handgun calls and often the handgun is never seen. It's typically 'in the coat,' and there probably never was a handgun … this sort of thing. But it tells you the potential of violence certainly exists. But we knew a handgun had been used and a [smoke] bomb was discharged, so we were ready. And then we knew another armed robbery [had] occurred in the town of Rockwood, just north of our town."

A few minutes later, the Guelph robbery was reported, with notes that the Guelph police were in pursuit.

"This was now sending a message to us that this individual means business, [that] we're not dealing with an isolated bank robbery where the person is not armed, where they've just handed over a note. We're dealing with an individual who's armed, means business, [has] robbed three banks, and [was] now exchanging gunfire with police officers in a pursuit."

Once the suspect left the Guelph area, police attempted to set up a series of roadblocks. Stennett set one up with two officers from the Aurora detachment of the OPP. Although information was relayed on police frequencies, there were different bands for each force. "It's difficult with different locations to get good transmissions," said Stennett. "The coordination was good and certainly will be [even] better in future."

Up at 32 Sideroad, Stennett and company only had about ten seconds to set up the roadblock according to provincial guidelines, which included an "out" that the suspect could use to prevent a collision. "The idea is to slow them down. A lot of suspects may terminate the pursuit right then and there. Obviously, in this case, we have to realize that this is an individual who has committed a series of crimes, he's well armed, he's already been in numerous exchanges of gunfire with police, and this person's not about to stop."

Sure enough, Hermann opened fire on the roadblock with a .357 Magnum before continuing, via the "out," past Stennett and company.

"I now became the lead vehicle in the pursuit," said Stennett. "We continued eastbound on 32 Sideroad."

That road is a standard concession, a hilly dirt road that had construction zones here and there. "Not the best road to be driving one hundred kilometres an hour in a police pursuit exchanging gunfire," Stennett explained. And by this time, he could hear what would become a steady background sound to the chase — the *whup whup whup* of an OPP helicopter, dispatched to follow Beier's car and keep it in sight, and to videotape the chase.

Then came a ninety-degree turn in the road, something Al knew about, but something for which Hermann was obviously unprepared. As Hermann made the turn, he "started to lose control of his vehicle and blew out his right front tire. But he regained control of his car and, as I came around the corner behind him, he fired off another three shots."

Luckily, none of the shots hit either Al or his car. "The feeling that I had during this entire pursuit and gunfire was [that] here is an individual who is in a pursuit that is in excess of 120 kilometres alone, which is significant just on its own. He's committed three serious crimes, and he's using weapons. He's discharging weapons toward the police, a lot of close calls, no doubt a lot of things could have gone the other way and we would have had police funerals. This was a situation where he was clearly not going to give up. He was going to fight to the end."

Al Stennett paused. It was quiet in the interview room; I could hear the movement of people outside and the muted chatter of police officers talking over cases, but inside the room the seriousness of what transpired was being replayed in Al Stennett's mind, and was evident in his voice as he continued. The part that rankles law enforcement officials like Stennett and others is the fact that when someone is running from the law, the police become faceless ciphers; their value as human beings, in the eyes of the criminal, drops to zero. In the face of pursuing police cars and the constant and unsettling presence of the helicopter up above, it was desperation time for Hermann.

"This person was extremely violent. He was trying to kill policemen," said Stennett. "Maybe he did have a death wish. He knew we were not going to go away; we were not going to let him get away with what he'd just done. He has a helicopter above him, police vehicles coming after him ..."

Hermann continued to travel at eighty or ninety kilometres an hour for some distance. "Although the [flat] tire had some effect on the car, it didn't stop him," Stennett said. Hermann tossed another smoke bomb out the window as he sped toward Rockside Road.

Al said his response to the situation was automatic: "This is why training is so important. You'll fall back on those skills you know best. One is keeping a good distance behind [the suspect], 'pacing, not chasing,' would be the term. You know gunfire is being exchanged, so you don't want to get too close."

At Rockside Road, just south of Olde Base Line Road, Hermann tossed out a tear gas canister, called *Clear Out*, that sent clouds of smoky fumes into the air. It was a move that would distract the police rather than impair them. Stennett recounted that the fine print on the canister later revealed it to be a "non-flammable riot control package for law enforcement only."

During testimony, discussion in the court focused on Hermann's alleged attempts at shooting to kill police officers. A major component of Hermann's defence was based on trying to differentiate between "shooting" and "shooting to kill."

Some testimony by officers who were on the scene was unclear about whether Hermann had intent to kill. Said Constable Jacinta of one confrontation, "The driver's door was left standing open and he had a gun in his hand and he began pointing it at us. I don't know [if he was pointing it] specifically at me, but it was pointing toward us and we started to bail out of the cars."

Staff Sergeant Groenendyk stated a similar case: "I had no evidence that [the gun] was pointing at me, no, but I know he was firing guns … I can't say that I saw the gun being aimed at me … I didn't feel that I was getting shot at directly, no."

Robert Cianci made similar observations. "The male had got out of the Lincoln, fired two shots at us, not in succession. He fired the first shot and there seemed to be a pause and then a second shot, and that's when I returned fire.… He was pointing the firearm down the road at us, and when somebody takes that deliberate aim and crouching position, they're shooting at you."

From Rockside, the chase continued onto Olde Base Line. It's a very hilly road with lots of twists and turns. Hermann was loaded to the hilt with ammunition, according to Stennett. "He's not running out of bullets. As a police officer, you're also keeping in the back of your mind that you've got limited resources at your disposal. You've got one .38 handgun with twelve rounds of ammunition and that's it. When it's gone, it's gone." Unlike in most police cars today, there was no shotgun in the vehicle; nothing more powerful than the standard-issue .38.

At Olde Base Line, a civilian car was idling at a stop sign, the driver dutifully waiting to go. Hermann exited the Lincoln and began walking toward the civilian's car. Immediately, Al could see a potential hostage-taking incident beginning. Hermann had a handgun in his right hand. Stennett screeched to a halt and threw open his door, going into the "high risk traffic stop" position, crouched behind the wheel of his car, right foot on the brake and the left foot holding the driver's door open. This created a V-shaped opening between the door and the A-pillar, the car body column between the windshield and the driver's door; braced against the A-pillar, an officer can open fire while using the car as a shield. Stennett credits the position with saving his life.

The civilian's car was a late-model Corsica. Stennett figured it was either Hermann's intent to kill the civilian and take his car, take him as a hostage, or just force him out of the car and then drive off in it. "I figure this is what's happening now, and I've got to make literally a split-second decision. Again, this is when your training and your experience come through. I yelled at him to get away from the civilian, and he turned and directed his attention at me, because now I'm his direct threat. And he turned and opened fire on me, directly toward me."

The distance was only about five metres. Hermann pounded out three rounds from a square-barrel .45 automatic, a switch from the .357. This wasn't the stuff of the movies, of extreme action in films like *Dirty Harry*, *Die Hard*, or *Scarface*. Forget the slow-motion drama and heady background music, this definitely was the stuff of heavy-duty gun blasts and the stench of spent gunpowder and dust layered against a metallic background rhythm of bullets pinging off cars, the chatter of the police radio, and the whooshing of the helicopter above.

"He's going to have between thirteen and seventeen rounds in his handgun against my six [remaining] rounds, so he's going to have the upper hand," added Stennett. "You're squaring off against somebody who's going to kill you. They're pointing their firearm at you; they're going to kill you. They've already discharged their weapon at you, they're discharging their weapon at you now … this person is going to kill you now. You think of absolutely nothing else but surviving this encounter. You'll do anything and everything to survive. I have to kill this man to survive or else he is going to kill me."

Shots are exchanged, with Stennett trying to aim his shots as far away from the civilian as possible. Even in close quarters, and with the adrenalin flowing, the accuracy deteriorates. "I've got a citizen over there to the left … but at the same time I've got to return fire." But the civilian, fortunately, was okay, and began driving away from the area after Al yelled at Hermann. But at that point Stennett was faced with a more pressing concern — an angry, focused, heavily armed assailant. In that situation, he told me, "You have tunnel vision. You have a direct threat in front of you and you're basically focusing on that threat and nothing else."

Al's ammunition was running out. As Hermann advanced on Al's vehicle, he pumped bullets at the officer with a cold, calculated, no-holds-barred attitude that prompted some officers to compare him to Arnold Schwarzenegger's Terminator, an indestructible mega-man. "Somehow you've got to pull through this," said Stennett. "You'll do anything to survive. Now, in this case, that meant returning fire. My ammunition was running out, this person was still advancing toward me, still discharging his firearm. The only solution ... was to run him over."

With two hands on the gun, Hermann "was taking a very professional combat advancement," says Stennett. "He was cool and collected and was doing what he had to do at that particular time. Of course, I was running out of ammunition and there was no time to reload ... it takes time [to reload]. You're nervous and [feel like] you're going to drop rounds."

Stennett continued. "I [had] no other solution but to run him over. I hit the gas and accelerated, but at the same instant that I did that, he turned and ended his assault toward me and started to go back to his car [sidestepping Stennett's vehicle], then commenced an assault at my car as I went by. He opened up a few rounds. I missed him with the car. I nosedived into a ditch that was about six and a half feet deep at about forty kilometres an hour."

The impact drove Stennett's head up against both his gun and the A-pillar. He was thrown out of the cruiser. Spilling out onto the ground, there was blood on his face and a gash in his leg from the bottom edge of the car door. He had landed on top of his gun and started to search frantically for it. He looked up toward the road, heard more gunfire [from the police officers that followed], and expected Hermann to come down after him. His thoughts were clear: "I've got to find my revolver. I'm on top of it, that's why I can't find it. At the same time I feel like I'm going to pass out." Suffering a concussion, Stennett looked for a safe place and began crawling toward a culvert under the road.

"I made the decision that it's time to escape, it's time to boogie through that hole at all costs. I start to crawl across the ditch; the entrance is eight feet away, which doesn't seem like much ... but unfortunately it's a big distance when all this [concussion] is going on. As I crawl across the side of the car, gunfire is still going and I hear a ping." A shot had gone through the hood of the car. "Somehow I've got to get through that ditch." He chuckled. "The funniest part of the whole thing is that I look into this culvert and it's wet and there's garbage and junk and I think to myself *God, I don't want to go in there, but I've got to go in there.* And then I think, *God, I hope I don't get stuck.*"

Hermann was in a raging gun battle now with the officers in the cars that followed behind Stennett. And it was at that moment that Stennett, ready to dive into the muck and filth to save his life, felt a strong hand latch onto his shoulder. "[I thought], *he's jumped into the ditch to take cover from all the gunfire and he's grabbed me and now he's going to throw a couple rounds into the back of my head so I'm not going to create any problems.*"

In fact, it was the hand of Stennett's patrol sergeant, Al McWhirter. "Just as I go in, that was when my patrol sergeant jumps in and grabs me by the shoulder to pull me back. I turned and saw the stripes of the uniform and knew that it was the police."

McWhirter had followed Stennett in the pursuit. He told him that Hermann had taken off again. "At that particular time you realize just what the hell has happened to you in the last ten seconds and you realize *Holy shit, you know, I've been shot at and I could be hit someplace.* They're telling me my leg is bleeding and I want to pass out. At the same time you're convinced that you've been hit."

Fortunately, it was only the gash from the door frame, an injury that required a few stitches later in hospital. But it was in the immediate aftermath, that lulling calm when he came to the realization that his job was done, and, he told me, "It's then that you start thinking about your family."

A total of forty-five rounds of ammunition were fired during the eight-second gunfight. "Eight seconds is not a long time, but it's a long time in a gunfight," said Stennett.

The pursuit continued south on McLaughlin Road. With several cruisers in pursuit, Hermann pulled to a stop after cresting a steep hill not far from the Olde Base Line intersection and exited the vehicle. The OPP helicopter overhead conveyed this information to the officers in pursuit. Staff Sergeant Groenendyk and Constable Jacinta of the Guelph Police Service stopped somewhere between thirty and seventy metres from Hermann. Groenendyk sought cover in a small ditch at the roadside as other officers from the OPP and Guelph detachment pulled up.

Hermann blasted away at the police, and they returned fire. Constable Jacinta noticed that Hermann was having problems with his gun; it appeared to have jammed. When Hermann got back into the Lincoln and continued along McLaughlin Road, OPP constables Glen Newell and Dan Erskine took the lead.

Hermann ran another roadblock, set up by Sergeant Robert Burridge of Peel Regional Police, who brought out a shotgun and was in the process of unfolding the stock of the gun when Hermann came driving through, firing at the sergeant. Burridge returned fire, but the recoil of the shotgun slammed the weapon back and into his mouth, causing injury. Hermann then took a couple of shots at Erskine and Newell, the bullets glancing off their windshield.

Turning onto King Street, Hermann then took a shot at a civilian van in front of him. He passed it, but was forced onto the shoulder of the road by Constable Dale Smewing of Peel Regional Police. As Hermann attempted to exit the Lincoln this time, his car was rammed from behind by Newell's cruiser, forcing it into the roadside ditch. Hermann got out of the car (with difficulty, as a farmer's fence impeded his progress) in time to see Constable Erskine get out of the cruiser. Erskine saw a gun, yelled at Hermann twice to drop it, then watched as Hermann pointed the gun directly at him and fired. Erskine returned fire, hitting Hermann in his midsection and in the right thigh. Hermann was also shot in the ankles, though some injuries were considered accidentally self-inflicted as he tried to scramble out of the Lincoln.

There, against a farmer's fence in rural Ontario, the chase finally ended; it ended in a way never intended by the bank robber, for as all bank robbers do, he had hoped for a clean escape. But during the chase-and-shoot gun battle, a death wish had been ignited in Hermann; it was a wish that would be denied. As he had said many times, he was made of tough stuff — he would survive his injuries, though they would leave him with nagging health issues.

Hermann was down, and the fight was over. The police approached cautiously. Underneath Hermann's leg was the .357 Magnum Smith & Wesson revolver; in the back of his pants was a .22-calibre semiautomatic handgun, and under the Lincoln's passenger seat was a .44 Magnum Ruger. In a sheath attached to his belt he carried a double-edged throwing knife. Ammunition was later found in the car — "a large quantity," the court heard — along with the money from that morning's robberies and stolen New Brunswick, New York, and Quebec licence plates. The radio in the Lincoln was tuned to the police band.

At 11:10 a.m. on that clear and mild autumn day, Hermann was arrested for attempted murder and taken to Peel Memorial Hospital for treatment of his injuries.

Hermann disagreed with the information provided by the police, which indicated that he was holding a gun when he was arrested. Whether or not it had any real bearing on the outcome of his trial, during my second interview with him, he vehemently disputed this testimony.

"I know 100 percent I didn't have a gun in my hand. I mean, you could see it on the [police video] tape. I had a glove, a black glove. I personally think you can see I didn't have a gun in my hand. I personally feel because I know I didn't have one.... [The police] want to see a gun in my hand. The whole situation in the end ... the police [were] so mad at me because so many cruisers chased me ... [and] the helicopter, so many shots [fired] at me, so many roadblocks. You just couldn't stop me, and I don't want to stop, period! I just don't want to stop. In the end they were so mad — two out of three times was called 'police is down' ... so, finally I was confronted by some police officer and he was so [angry] ... he shot ..."

He looked away at that point, his energy depleted for the moment.

The man who shot Hermann Beier lived on a quiet street in Guelph. And he wouldn't talk about the shooting. His son answered the phone when I called in late 1993, then passed it on to his dad. Constable Erskine's voice was steady, but thick and tired. He was enjoying a day off before his next shift began on the weekend. He sounded as if he still carried much emotional baggage. He refused to be interviewed. "But maybe I'll talk after I'm retired," he told me.

"When is that?" I asked.

"Maybe next year." Even in his refusal he was pleasant; he thanked me for the call and hung up.

Other officers involved in the chase and the shootouts said Erskine had been deeply, profoundly affected by what happened the morning of October 31, 1991. And he was certainly not saying anything to anyone about it. At least not at that time.

9

Aftermath

Detective Liz O'Donnell, an eleven-year member of the OPP (eight with the Caledon detachment, three of those years with its crime unit) made the arrest, cuffing a defiant, bloodied Hermann after he fell to the ground with six bullet holes in his leg, hip, and stomach, as well as injuries to his ankles. O'Donnell also served as the investigating officer in an inquiry that lasted seven months. She was left with boxes and boxes of transcripts and records of evidence, she said.

When I interviewed O'Donnell, I thought she had the look of a street-wise, duty-toughened female cop — she reminded me of Kathleen Turner in the movie *V.I. Warshawski*. She was about five foot nine, and the day I met her she was wearing a chartreuse business suit with square shoulders and a sensible skirt. Her not-quite-blond hair was styled in an easy-to-manage perm, and she wore little makeup. She didn't laugh easily, either, though she did offer me the occasional wry smile if she favoured a particular remark or observation. She joked around with her male colleagues with an "I'm not a man but I can get along with the boys" attitude familiar to women working in tough, male-dominated environments.

Though an active participant in the chase, O'Donnell didn't remember the sense of danger that the front-line cops felt: "We were far enough back that it was like watching television from the safety of your chair."

"There are lots of things that happen in a short period of time during a chase," she said. "I thought at the time, this guy thinks he's the Terminator. He thinks he's invincible."

It was, at the time, the longest police car chase in Canadian history, according to police.

The effects of stressful situations such as the chase and shootout can manifest themselves in participants as Post-Traumatic Stress Disorder (PTSD). While some officers tried to find ways of coping with the ordeal, either on their own or with the help of police employee assistance programs, O'Donnell explained that she had an advantage because she was doing the investigation. She could work through it, examining the chase and parsing it into the smallest of details, and this helped her to ease through the emotional challenges. Besides, she said, "He only pointed a gun at me. He never fired at me."

O'Donnell told me few people understand the deadly seriousness of the actions that took place that day. Just because cops are not killed is no reason to think it's not a very serious situation, she said. "We had bullet holes in windshields and [police officers] with glass shards down their necks. It's a really tough job for a police officer."

In her testimony before the court, O'Donnell emphasized the depth of the circumstances. "It was ... very dangerous," she told the preliminary inquiry before Judge T. Wolder in Brampton on September 4, 1992, of the moments that Hermann stopped to confront police. There were blind spots on the road where it twisted and turned on its way from Guelph to the rolling hills of Caledon. Officers were following each other via radio transmissions, trying to use as much information from the OPP helicopter as possible to determine Hermann's position and his actions. "Had it not been for the ... helicopter pilot giving that transmission, we ... would have gone over the crest of the hill just to be blind-sided by what would be ... an ambush situation."

Speaking about the confrontation between Hermann and Constable Dan Erskine of the Guelph detachment of the OPP, the officer who delivered the shots that felled the suspect, O'Donnell recounted the overriding sense of danger that was prevalent.

"I was very concerned because he [Erskine] was ... out in the open and the driver of the Lincoln just came out shooting and it ... was really frightening. I could not see Constable Erskine's hand or his gun because his back was to me. I could only see him standing perfectly straight beside the cruiser and I heard the sound of gunshots. I don't recall if I saw any smoke or anything like that from the … driver of the Lincoln's handgun, but I just remember knowing that that's who was shooting … and then the next thing I saw … he [Beier] went down to the ground face first."

Another officer who helped in the robbery investigation, and spoke to me on condition of anonymity, was convinced that Hermann had a superiority complex, or inferiority complex, depending on how you want to look at it: "He really doesn't know the seriousness of his crimes."

That officer and another offered insight during an afternoon conversation. To say that they were angry at Hermann would be a vast understatement; many months later, they seethed when speaking about him, incensed at him for giving them a really hard time and angry at how he forced police officers into a stressful, life-threatening situation.

"He was very well-organized," the first one said. He leaned forward, hands flexed, fingers tightened. "He's bold as brass. He has great opinions of himself that he's a bit superior — to say the least."

That suggestion of a superiority complex rings clear in every conversation I had with police. And it was made clear during courtroom procedures, when Hermann, upon entering the courtroom, bowed, martial arts style, to the empty judge's chair. He treated everyone else in the courtroom as underlings, while only the judge was given the status of an equal. I'm thinking he may have just picked this up from the lawyers, who bow, in keeping with tradition, out of respect for the Crown.

But his attitude? According to police, it was that of a kid playing Ninja games.

"I basically think that it was all fun and games for Hermann," the officer told me. "He was playing games. He was having fun. He never thought he was going to get caught. He thought that he was tougher, faster, and better than the police. If he hadn't got greedy and hit that third bank, it would have been a couple of days before we got him."

A fellow officer said that Hermann had a strong desire to control situations around him. "He has to be in control of the situation, and if that means manipulating someone, so be it."

On Hermann's ability with the martial art of Hapkido, one officer discounted Hermann's claim that he was an expert as downright laughable.

A trophy that Hermann received in a competition was awarded to him because, during the four-man competition, the first opponent was disqualified for breaking Hermann's jaw. The next opponent was injured and dropped out, the officer said. Hermann was too slow, putting himself in a position to have his jaw broken. He barely made it past the third opponent, so the win came almost by default.

The officer considered it "a joke" that Hermann ran a martial arts studio in Alliston. "He had that big trophy up on the mantle, and at what cost? I guess a broken jaw was worth it to him."

Another officer reiterated the notion that if Hermann was self-taught, he had a poor teacher. "I'm not saying that he couldn't have taught himself. I mean, that's what he did. But he wasn't very good at it."

Carmen Knapp, who went on to become a detective-inspector with the OPP in Kingston, was the investigation's case manager. His voice was tight, succinct. There was no question in the minds of the police that the October 31 heists would have been "just a start" for Hermann. "He had a list of about twenty-four banks in the front seat of his car," said Knapp. "Out of the top four banks, three had been robbed that day. He had full intentions to rob quite a list of banks."

Knapp had spent twenty-eight years as a police officer, including time on plainclothes duty and as a drug enforcement officer. He was clearly appalled by Hermann's behaviour. "What did he think he was on, a picnic, an outing? It always amazes me with these criminals how their attitude changes after they get caught. I got the sense it seemed like an adventure. He was on an adventure; he wasn't going to earn money the regular way. Sooner or later it would have certainly led to someone's death."

In a four-page report, psychiatrist Dr. Robert Coulthard of Mississauga said that Hermann's behaviour resulted from several factors in his life: "He was faced with many disappointments with regard to achievement. He strived to earn the respect of others. And he faced several serious losses."

The report stated that events such as the death of his mother, who passed away in Hermann's arms in 1971, affected him tremendously. So did his father's treatment of him. His father was a strict disciplinarian, described by Hermann as "150 percent policeman."

And the report reads like a primer for disappointment: The youngest of four children, Hermann was married in 1971 and had four children — at the time of the robberies, all four were in their thirties and living in Germany. Hermann had finished grade eight and then gone on to trade school until grade twelve. Active in sports, he grew to dislike alcohol and drugs and didn't smoke. But there were always pressures to complete dreams and goals. He attempted to join various police forces several times, but was rejected. A series of bad personal relationships did not help, and Hermann tended to move from one relationship to the next. These changes were usually accompanied by financial difficulties. The death of a dog, and later the birds at his sanctuary, added to his depression.

He told Dr. Coulthard that his motivation for the robberies was to get money to pay off his debts.

The psychiatrist's report also found that Hermann was subconsciously suicidal — he had a "death wish," as previously mentioned, which led him into the open confrontations with police during the Halloween chase.

The summation stated that Hermann was rigid and proud, but also pleasant and cooperative, with bright–average intelligence; but he was preoccupied with past losses and failures. The report also concluded that there was "no antisocial behaviour evident" in Hermann, although it cautioned that there was no way to predict Hermann's needs in prison with regard to possible treatment, and there was no way to predict his behaviour once he was released.

10

INCARCERATION

FOLLOWING HIS ARREST, HERMANN'S EXPERIENCE WITH THE PROCESS of the law was overwhelming. From guarded hospital rooms to holding cells to detention centres, courthouses, and penitentiaries, it was all much more difficult to deal with than he had anticipated — the iron hand of law enforcement, he felt, was crushing him. And on top of this, his mind was riddled with regrets and doubts about the future: "[When] I woke up, and when my mind starting working again, in hospital ... my first question was whether somebody was hurt. I didn't want to hurt anybody."

Once in jail, Hermann claimed he was victimized by police and corrections officials because of his thick German accent. "This has happened in the hospital, from the police, in the detention centre ... but I never said things about my case, it was just the way I talked. I tried to get something out and they twisted my words around. That is not fair, but what can I do? This is the system today."

Hermann spent time at both the Metro East and Metro West Detention Centres (now the Toronto East and West Detention Centres), located in the suburbs of Toronto. The Metro West Detention Centre, where he spent fifteen months while awaiting his time in court, had an especially intimidating atmosphere. "It's high security. This [Millhaven, where he was located during the interview] is maximum [security]. But I would call a detention centre a jail. The [detention centre] is more than maximum, because whatever you do, you have always a guard beside you. Here [in Millhaven], I sit alone, I go pick up my books from the library, I go alone to the chapel, I go alone to the gym. You are not alone at the detention centre."

He paused to collect his thoughts, then continued: "Canadian law, or any law, says [you are] innocent until proven guilty. This is the Canadian law, but in the real world you are guilty until you prove your innocence. You get treated [like you're guilty]. Not personally me, because again, I'm an easygoing person."

Hermann described himself as a model inmate: "I don't scream. The guards do their job more or less — not all of them, but most. They have the key; I have to take the oath. I'm a person who took the oath my whole life. I was in the military; I take the oaths of the martial arts, I take the oath sometimes at home. I make my own and keep my own oaths. Being clean, organized. So, you have to keep your oaths, but some guards don't like it when you are being a nice person, because they can't handle it."

He suggested that the guards revelled in the uncertainty of inmates, in keeping them on edge: "I can tell you a few stories about women guards, about men guards. They are amazed by how I talk to them: *Please. Thank you.* When you go in a detention centre, you get treated, what I would call and I've heard other people say is, worse than an animal. How you live, how often you get a change of clothes. Meals sometimes pushed under the door. I would not treat my animals, my own dogs I had [like that] ... I was treating them better than I was treated in a detention centre. My birds, for example, it's different, but I cleaned them, I gave them food. This is how it is and ... if you are a wise person, and you do nothing against them, they find something to tease you [about], to provoke you, to make you scream."

That may be true; however, a former inmate who spent four "intense" days with Hermann in the hospital of the Metro East Detention Centre said that during that time in February 1992, Hermann displayed an interesting side of his personality. He told me that at times Hermann was charming, at times moody; at all times he was "definitely turned on to the Bible." While talking candidly about Hermann, the former inmate, who we'll call "Bob," refused to allow his name to be used. Bob was described by Hermann as a "close friend." Bob didn't absolutely dispute this claim.

Photo by John Cooper

Hermann was incarcerated in the Metro (now Toronto) East Detention Centre after his arrest. Anger, violence, and uncertainty were all endemic to the facility, where inmates waited for their trials to begin or end.

"A man who would be in his particular circumstances would certainly feel that anyone who would speak to him would be a friend," said Bob.

At the time, Hermann was receiving treatment for his gunshot wounds.

"At times he resembled a — how will I put it — a high tension wire with a short circuit," said Bob. "And other times he was very calm and very meek. He was relying very much on newfound religion and the Bible for comfort. Some individuals use it as a genuine crutch. Others use it as a stepping stone to free them."

Was Hermann just scamming the system? Did he want to use his religious beliefs as leverage for an earlier release, better privileges? "I would say in his case it would be genuine," replied Bob. "It was something newfound in his life. At no time did he ever advocate to me or anyone else that they should become religious zealots like him. Usually those with a religious aspect who are phony want to push it."

Hermann revealed other interesting aspects of his personality to Bob. For instance, he called himself a Dominion Marksman: "He stated in conversation that the Dominion Marksman is a high standing in Canada for revolver competition. As a matter of fact, he stated that whatever he pointed a gun at, he hit."

Bob said he can't understand why this claim wasn't brought out in court. "If Hermann was such an excellent marksman, couldn't the court see that if he had wanted to kill any of the police officers during the October 31 chase, he could have?" (Later, in a response to the question via letter, Hermann said he knew nothing of the "Dominion Marksman" title. "What does that mean?" he asked.)

Is Hermann as much of a charmer as he claims to be? Yes, said Bob. But Hermann, he said, could also be moody and irritable: "He's a very charming individual with an obstinate Teutonic streak. If he does not get his own way, he becomes somewhat unbearable. He goes into a mental shell or cocoon-like structure where he sits and tries to figure out an angle where he's going to beat the system."

Hermann's own lack of understanding of the penal system may have had adverse effects as well, Bob said: "When you're incarcerated, there [are] certain rules and no one gets any special treatment despite the severity of the offence. And at times he thought it was his God-given right that he be treated in a preferential style." He provided an example: "You've got a great number of people wanting to use the telephone and when one individual wants it at a particular point in time over and above everyone else, he sticks out like a sore thumb."

Hermann didn't exhibit any violence in Metro East, Bob told me. "I never saw any form of violence in the man. He was like a little pussycat."

Hermann said that it was at Metro West that he "rediscovered" religion. He told me a strong belief in God and Jesus helped him stay alive and hopeful for the future. He said he was deeply religious; a plastic crucifix and rosary hung prominently around his neck. Although he said he was Protestant, he attended Catholic services in prison. As he spoke, he touched the crucifix tentatively, as if continually reminding himself of some unspoken message that it contained for him alone. It didn't appear to be an act for the benefit of an audience of one.

Metro (now Toronto) West Detention Centre. Hermann spent fifteen months in the facility, where he rediscovered religion and, according to a priest at the facility, was trying honestly to come to terms with his life.

Photo by John Cooper

Catholic priest Reverend Tom Pillisch of Metro West had contact with Hermann occasionally during his time at the centre. He told me over the phone in 1993 that he believed Hermann was trying to come to terms with himself. Pillisch believed that his acceptance of religion was sincere. "I only had one deep discussion with him in all the time he stayed here. And his concern was that he was trying to get married here [to a former girlfriend]," he said. He later allowed that there were several less intense discussions, though those were still serious enough for their content to be reserved for the confidence of the clergy; about these, Pillisch offered no details.

The plans for the marriage he mentioned fell through, but Reverend Pillisch was convinced that Hermann's faith was true. "He's a serious man. I think he was very sincere. I think he had a very troubled life, much like many people who come here. Perhaps one of the ironies of all this is that he comes from a very disciplined background. His father was a prison warden. Hours before he left here, he came to chapel and he gave a full confession. I think he found himself; he has to find the original person who was lost during the problems he had. I pray that at last he has come together."

That coming together may be a long process. Hermann discovered some unsettling realities of cruelty and contempt while in Metro West. "In the detention centre, some guards … it's like for them it is a challenge, for them it is fun to tease you. You start screaming, you start touching them [by "touch," one assumes throwing punches or pushing them], and they just beat you up. The blue button [the emergency response switch] is hit … ten or fifteen guards beat you up."

Hermann said he was thankful that it didn't happen to him. He also told me he was aware that other inmates thought him to be an arrogant individual: "My mind and my body are so, so strong, I feel they cannot hurt me [so] I just walk away. In this case, I'm more mature than some guards, but I never had a problem with any guards, I never screamed, but I wrote many letter[s] to the correction centre head office. I talked to the superintendent … because the system, it's wrong somehow in the detention centre what they do with you. I saw guards teasing other inmates that were more explosive than me, just to have the fun to beat them up … provoke them to do it and throw them right away in the hole [solitary confinement]; this is the punishment without any privilege, without any clothes … no mattress. In the daytime, no reading, no cigarettes, nothing…. In a detention centre it is not human at all."

He also missed the fresh air while in the detention centre. "I'm an outgoing person and I like to go out in the fresh air, walking around in the fresh air all day, but there you are locked up, you always have somebody with you [and] for everything you have to ask, for everything you have to request, and you don't know if you get it. I know that sometimes, not always in my case, but other inmates' things end up in the garbage.

"You ask for something, they have no time. Like if you have to have a pencil sharpened because you have nothing in your cell. The guards are supposed to be there to serve you because you're in jail, but they say 'I don't have time.' They don't do this, they don't do that. This is to provoke you to do something wrong. I say 'Okay, if you don't want to do it now, maybe in half an hour I ask you again.' So I walk away. I don't stay, I don't

Photo by John Cooper

Exercise yard at Metro (now Toronto) West Detention Centre, where Hermann said there was no privacy, a lack of fresh air, and the guards could be cruel and tormenting.

say anything. In the meantime, in my case, wherever I went, people or the guards recognize me, realize I'm a nice person and I have, I wouldn't say, privileges, but they let me out to sharpen my pencil."

Reminiscing like this got Hermann into a thoughtful mood: "I met a lot a people in the [Metro East] detention centre. Whatever they got charged with, they are nice people. You have to realize ... why this person ended up in jail. I'm not talking repeat break and enter, drug dealers, I'm not talking these people, they come and go in jail, in and out, they have two homes, outside and inside.... I'm talking about people like me ... a first-timer. Some people already two or three times in jail, but they are nice people. A young fellow I met — he is now in here [Millhaven] — he gets four and a half years. I talk to him for days because he is my room partner and he tried to go out in society, but society would not have him. The parole officer would not help him, the parents would not help him anymore; he had a girlfriend, she helped, but this was not enough. He needed really professional help. Boom, he ends up in jail again. Like

I said at the beginning, police watch you because you were one time in jail; they watch you all the time. Just a little thing you do wrong, *Bingo!* You end up [back] in jail. I'm scared that when I come out some day on parole, I know for [a] fact that because of the shootout I will be watched by the police like a five-million-dollar diamond. They'll watch me wherever I go, whatever I do, still missing $130,000 that I don't have. I don't know where the money is. I don't have this money. See, that is another reason: if I had $130,000, why would I have to do the second time a bank robbery? I just wanted enough to pay off my debts, peanuts.

"Now in jail I learned to read the Bible. I'm Christian for all my life, but I never was so close to God as I am now. People have the Bible in the hand in court and swear by God to tell the truth and nothing but the truth, and the moment they put the Bible down and open up the mouth, out come just lies. It doesn't matter who it is, but if you follow the police officers' statements, you just shake your head."

Hermann looked at the walls around him; watched as the dust motes danced in the sunlight that filtered through the louvred slats. The light from the afternoon sun was dimming. We could hear the echoes of fellow inmates. The atmosphere there punctuated and distorted ordinary, everyday sounds — muffled conversations, a dropped pen, footsteps — into something surreal. In Hermann's creased face, I suddenly saw his bravado beginning to slip away as he groped for an explanation, a brave statement that would convey that he was used, that somebody, somewhere, somehow must have set him on the wrong path.

"I was sixteen months in [jail] and the judge said, 'If you want to carry on to have a trial it could be up to another year until you're finished' — another year in the detention centre. Then I might get more time because of all the pain of the people [testifying at] the trial. So, slowly you get pushed into the corner, not me only, but other inmates or criminals too … people get held in a detention centre, I guess sometimes on purpose. I'm not saying because we don't have enough judges or you don't have enough courts to make speeding up a little bit. I feel sometimes people get pushed and held in the detention centre to squeeze them to say 'yes I did it,' put them for so many years in a penitentiary. That is not fair either. I felt it was not so in the time I was outside, but now I'm in the system, other people tell me, 'I know,' [but] you cannot know. I want the truth, what really happened. Always in my life I always tell the truth, I always be straight. I don't go this way or this way just for my own good sake. No. I get hurt. Fine. In my life I get hurt a thousand times, not in criminal matters, but emotionally, whatever. That doesn't bother me so much, you get over it … here you try to be fair and honest, but the people around you, no matter who it is — the police and other people — are twisting and turning the real truth, to make you wild."

Hermann was sentenced to thirteen years. He would be eligible for UTA (unescorted temporary absence) beginning in April 1995 (at that time, because of his appeal, this had been denied), day parole in December 1996, and full parole in June 1997. If he made parole, he would be fifty-six years old.

Hermann spent most of his time at Millhaven — twenty-two hours a day — in his cell, although he later earned the privilege of greater freedom through time spent on the work range.

After the interview was done, I had some time on my hands. I spoke with several guards, to get a sense of what it was like in Millhaven, the day-to-day routine of the place. A beefy head guard with short-cropped hair the colour of carrots, about five foot eight and close to three hundred pounds, told me that maintaining control of the situation was the guards' main concern. He frankly looked like the kind of guy who enjoyed "the control thing," someone who didn't mind — maybe even relished — the use of force.

We went on a short walking tour of one of the ranges where the inmates lived. There were rows of steel doors, each with a small window at the top; behind each was a cell. The space was artificially lit; sections of the hallway were separated by sliding, electronically operated barred doors. The vertical bars had a curving, rococo look to them, almost decorative. On one of the ranges, the guard opened a cell door that opened into a spartan room that measured about six by ten feet. It had two bunks, a desk at one end, that solid steel door (no clanking tin cups, no Cool Hand Luke peering out from behind bars here), and a louvred window that looked out into an exercise yard.

"You wanna be locked in there to get a feel for it?" he asked me, laughing. His laugh was throaty and unsettling. I got the feeling that if I went in there, I'd be waiting a hell of a long time before someone came to let me out. The guard's idea of a joke, perhaps.

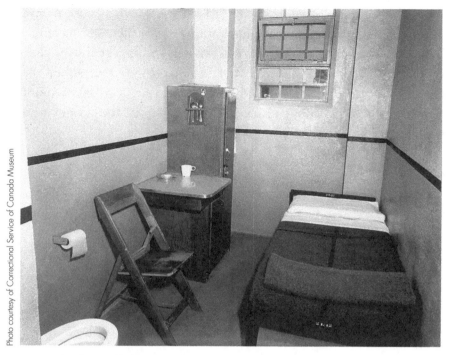

A typical cell in Millhaven is about six by ten feet, and about as basic as you can get. Cells have solid steel doors, but the window ensures that at least a bit of natural light enters the cell.

Photo courtesy of Correctional Service of Canada Museum

"No thanks," I said.

I looked through the cell window. Dun-coloured sparrows tweeted and flitted about the yard outside. I asked the guard what the inmates were like. He laughed again: "Some of these guys are okay, but some of them are fucking assholes."

When I asked him what Hermann was like, the guard wheezed out a chuckle, then smiled and crinkled his eyes as if to say "mind your own business."

After our interview, I received many letters from Hermann. In all of them, he talked about his hopes, fears, and concerns. For instance, he told me he wanted to study computers in prison. In another letter, he told me he wanted to move to Brazil to breed budgies when he got out.

One other plan Hermann talked about was a fundraising roller-blade skate from one coast of Canada to the other, "like Rick Hansen did with the wheelchair," he said. "Or before him, what is the name? Terry Fox. I have it in my mind just for myself, for my own challenge. Now I can do it, or I will do it, to raise money to support abused children and women. I talked already to a few chaplains in here and in the detention centre, and they found the idea is great. Now is my point first to get fixed my hip, and second I need help … to find out who supplies rollerblades."

11

ALLISTON: BIG FROG, SMALL POND

IN 1993, ALLISTON, ONTARIO, POPULATION 6,200, WAS (AND STILL IS) A quiet little town tucked into the hills south of Barrie. It is still mainly a farming community, but is increasingly becoming the home to manufacturing businesses ranging from textile producers to pharmaceutical firms to cars.

Like other small towns in Ontario, you know you're approaching Alliston's core when you pass a Becker's milk store, the Chrysler, Ford, or GM dealership (take your pick), and the ubiquitous Tim Hortons doughnut shop. Businesses breed along the main roads, gathering into an orderly herd that spreads out along it; the herd thickens as you enter the town. It becomes older, more sedate, slackening its pace as it hits the main drag.

Alliston has a bustling downtown area and many of the businesses have retained nineteenth- and early twentieth-century façades. It's one long street, unencumbered by the forceful buy-from-us urgency of the big-name stores or the banal might of the big box operations — heck, the biggest name back in 1993 was still Woolworth's, the original five-and-dime. It was a place where the local movie theatre was still called the Bijou and the ice cream parlour wasn't a Baskin Robbins.

As I drove through town that day in 1993, I observed a flow of pedestrian traffic, people wearing the ubiquitous baseball cap, the headgear sheltering the sunburned, weather-lined faces of farm folk and boys on the street, about a fifty-fifty split between "Pickseed" and "Chicago Bulls."

The Boyne River, a tributary of the Nottawasaga, flows through Alliston. The town was founded in 1847 by William Fletcher, who had lived in the area since 1821. Fletcher named Alliston for his hometown in Yorkshire, England.

William and his son John built a log shanty on the site; the next year the pair put up a frame house and a sawmill on the river's north side. The business took off, bringing much attention to the enterprise and triggering settlers and trades people to move into the area. William recognized the potential and added a grist mill in 1853. By 1858, a post office had been opened, with George Fletcher (William's son) as postmaster. George went on to publish the *Alliston Star*, which became the *Herald* in 1871 and, when I visited, was still being published every week.

Alliston also had a booming church-going community: Back in 1854, the Methodists had a church, and in the 1860s, William and John Buyers built a school and a church (called Knox Church, torn down in 1915 to make way for a bigger facility). St. John's Wesleyan Methodist Church was built in 1872. St. Paul's Roman Catholic Church joined the community in 1876, the year that Alliston's first Anglican Church was built.

When looking at the town's most famous residents, two immediately come to mind: Sir Frederick Banting and T.P. Loblaw. Perhaps Alliston's most famous son was Banting, the co-discoverer of insulin and winner of a Nobel Prize. A man with a storied history, Banting isolated insulin back in 1924 and was known for being a challenging man and often difficult to get along with. As for Loblaw, he was the town's most famous benefactor; the grocery-store founder provided funding for the construction of Stevenson Memorial Hospital in 1928.

By 1993, Alliston's most notorious (former) resident was Hermann Beier. Like Banting, he didn't always get along well with others, but unlike the brilliant scientist, he made no great discoveries. But like Loblaw, he had an entrepreneurial spirit. He was possessed of determination, strong ideas, and a desire to see his plans become reality.

When I visited Alliston, the town was still growing. In January 1992, its administration had come under the umbrella of the larger municipal jurisdiction of the Town of New Tecumseth. Politics in a small town is an example of networking in action. Big-city politicians may deliver platitudes far away from their ridings; they might spend

Photo courtesy of Museum of the Boyne, Alliston

Downtown Alliston, 1990. In the late 1980s, Hermann moved to the town of about 15,000, which he thought was an ideal location for his handyman business. He hatched some ambitious business plans while living there.

one day a week listening to constituents' concerns. Their success is as much the product of careful planning and marketing as being a friendly, committed representative.

Not so with small-town politicians. Their visibility, and accountability, increases as the population decreases — the more you are seen by your constituents, the more accessible and accountable you must be.

To that end, Hermann felt he fit the mould of the small-town politician.

Deputy Town Clerk Pat Middlebrook remembered Hermann filing his intent to run in the November 12, 1991, elections as a Ward One councillor. Hermann was an active part of community events and showed up at Town Hall on a variety of business, generally associated with his health club and budgie shop.

"He registered and he filed his nomination papers that qualified him to run in the election," said Pat. "He was arrested prior to the election, [but] the time had passed [and] he couldn't be removed from the ballot. But he was popular and he did get some votes."

Hermann, despite his incarceration, received a total of 107 votes.

It was a Saturday morning when I visited Alliston. Bored teenagers wandered along the street, subtly checking the cars that drove by (might be Mom or Dad) as they took a few furtive drags on the cigarettes they carefully cupped in their hands.

I passed streets with names like Wellington and Victoria and Dufferin and Church. These were in the residential areas, lined with one-hundred-year-old maple trees that towered over strong and stable two-storey homes. The streets intersected at precise right angles on either side of the east-west main drag. A concrete bridge, its metal guard rail showing signs of rust, reached across a slow-moving river. This was Alliston, the perfect small pond for a big frog. Or maybe for a small frog who wants to appear larger.

After making a wrong turn onto a side street, I eased across a bridge over the Boyne River and pulled over to ask a teenager heading to the town core for directions to the library. She eyed me cautiously. I was thinking the influence of mass media on teenagers can't be all bad; she had an "I don't know you" look of suspicion on her face. I assumed she knew all about the Paul Bernardo/Karla Homolka trials — the big media event of the time — and the luring of young teenage girls into cars and the awful things that happened afterward. Even tucked away in this environment of summer's-day rural ambience, she was still wary.

But conditioning won out (this is rural Ontario after all and, true to the cliché, people in small towns tend to be friendly), and she gave me directions. "Next to the theatre," she told me, waving her hand in the general direction.

Alliston Memorial Library was one of the more modern looking buildings on the block. The librarian was a substantial woman, her age buried somewhere around forty under a mass of jet black hair and a face free of makeup; her relaxed friendliness whispered a litany of health, of whole wheat muffins, organically-grown vegetables, rose hip tea, and Birkenstock sandals. She told me she was born and raised in Alliston, but only returned a year before from "out west"; she remembered hearing her parents talk about Hermann Beier.

After I told her my reason for being there, she headed into the back room and returned with a stack of *Alliston Herald*s. She then proceeded to bring out two more stacks. "You're welcome to go through them," she said, and then added with a smile, "Please take as much time as you want."

No more than a half-dozen patrons littered the library that day, leaning into newspapers and books or shuffling down the aisles in haphazard fashion, seeking comfort from the heat of the day, or looking for something to do to pass the time. I spread the papers out on a heavy black table. A couple of tables away, a man who looked to be in his seventies wheezed as he leafed through a magazine. He looked at me, as if trying to recognize me from somewhere, then returned to his reading.

I pored over the papers. A story by reporter Vicki Wirkkunen had appeared a week after Hermann's arrest, with the kicker "Alliston man in hospital after being shot by police" and the headline "Beier Facing Attempted Murder Charges."

The article began: "A local man known for his handyman services, budgie breeding, and mastery of martial arts has now gained more notoriety. Police are dredging up files from the past in their ongoing investigations after a 50-year-old Alliston man took officers from a number of forces on a high-speed chase across a small section of southern Ontario on Thursday ..."

It then went on to say, "A turn of events [that] led to Hermann Beier currently resting in a Peel Memorial Hospital bed under Ministry of Correctional Services guard began early last Wednesday."

Two photographs accompanied the article; one was of Hermann fixing a metal bracket with a wrench. The cutline read: "Opening business. Hermann Beier has opened several businesses since moving to Alliston. He has been involved with a karate school, weight training/fitness centre, and most recently a health weight-loss clinic." The second photo was a promotional, studio-shot piece of Hermann in an elaborate, trim martial arts outfit, striking a Hapkido pose.

The paper ran a few short items in subsequent issues, basically updates, including a November 20, 1991, story headed "Beier Faces 85 Charges." The articles were brief and to the point.

I looked through two years of newspapers — two years of farm auctions, ploughing matches, and reports from town council — in search of local news stories relating to the robberies. I had expected a plethora of news stories, in-depth analyses and the like, but I found that interest in the case was as shifting and uncertain as farm prices. There had been no rally for Hermann, no friends pledging to stick by him through the proverbial thick and thin. Hermann, and the memory of him, seemed to have just come and gone. I re-stacked the newspapers and returned them to the front desk. The black-haired woman gave me a warm smile as I left.

I got back in my car and drove along Dufferin Street South. The houses were soon replaced by small business malls. The Dufferin Street South Business Park, which once housed Hermann's businesses, was a squat group of small grey units, geometric, tightly built cubes that were home to local commercial and light industrial companies.

I ordered coffee at a down-on-its-heels sandwich shop anchoring one end of the little plaza, and asked the taciturn young man behind the counter if he knew anything about the businesses in the mall. He turned toward me, his thick glasses slightly askew, avoiding eye contact. He sensed my presence as opposed to seeing me. "Nope," he said.

"Do you know anything about Hermann Beier?"

"Nope."

"Know the name of the manager of this plaza?"

"Nope."

I scrambled for something else to say.

"Where is the library?" I asked him dumbly.

Now that was a question he could handle. Suddenly animated, he offered me not one, but three different routes to the library, then reached for a napkin and detailed a crude map for me, a jumble of lines on the textured surface; little blots of blue here and there indicated the library and major intersections.

I left the sandwich place and walked over to take a look at the location of Hermann's old shops. Between signs for Williamson Automotive (formerly Harlequin Place) and Proline Mechanical Inc. (the health and fitness centre) was one crumbling red-on-white marquee announcing HERMANN'S POOL & DARTS HALL. But the word *pool* had started flaking off and so it appeared to read HERMANN'S OL & DARTS HALL.

It was ironic that almost two years after the fact, the advertising for Hermann's ill-fated pool hall, which never even got off the ground, was still hanging, while his other businesses had been replaced. I took a look inside and saw several filing cabinets, a couple of desks, and a personal computer. It appeared to be a business setting with a brisk and busy look to it. I speculated that it was perhaps being used by one of the other businesses in the plaza.

Photo by John Cooper

By 1993, the deteriorating sign on his Pool & Darts club marked the end of Hermann's time in Alliston; He was already facing years of prison time for his bank robberies, though many in the town remembered him fondly.

During his years there, Hermann had gotten to know many people in and around Alliston. A young woman named Cheryl, from the nearby hamlet of Loretto, met him in May 1988 through a work placement program at Seneca College called Working Skills for Women. It was a six-month course held at the community college's Newmarket campus. She had a two-week placement with Hermann, after which she became a full-time employee at his handyman business, doing mainly wallpapering and painting. The job lasted a year and a half.

It was a consistent, steady job. "I never had to worry about getting paid," she told me.

Other employees didn't feel the same, I discovered. One stated off the record that Hermann operated "on a shoestring budget. He didn't have a full grasp of some of the jobs he had to do." Still, the former employee admitted that "he had great people skills and he could talk people into getting something done." She told me that several jobs were left uncompleted and there was a memorable small claims court battle with a customer.

Perhaps Hermann's biggest problem was that he was often an absentee boss, the former employee said. "Hermann, being a boss, should have been on the job site, showing off his knowledge and seeing that things were done. But he would say, 'This is what has to be done,' and then he would take off, leaving the job site to shop for pieces of lumber and other materials when that [job] should have been left to his employees."

Cheryl said that Hermann's masculine persona was as vital a tool as his hammer and saw. "He was very macho, particularly with his martial arts skills," she said. "That's the way he came across to women. He presented a picture of himself as a man about town. I always kind of thought that he wanted to make something of himself before he died. Despite it [the bank robberies] being illegal, you do remember [the good that] he did."

He also made it clear to women when he liked them. Cheryl was the recipient of a pass from Hermann. "At one point he wanted me to go to California with him, but I laughed it off."

Was he aggressive, as others have said? "I really don't think so," said Cheryl. "He was very charming. I think that if he had stayed within his line of what he could do, he would have been successful. He used to work for [kitchen cabinet manufacturer] Canarc Kitchens. He was very good at tiling. And his budgies … he was very bright when it came to his budgies."

For Emanuel Zammit, Hermann was a man with unquestioned leadership qualities. When I spoke with Zammit, he was living in the country with his common-law wife Darlene, about fifteen kilometres west of Alliston. Both he and Darlene had attended Hermann's fitness centre: "Darlene worked out [at the centre] and I took Hapkido."

Relaxed and easy-going over the phone, Zammit talked in friendly, open terms about Hermann. "We keep in touch," he told me, and even over the phone I sensed a genuine respect for Hermann.

Zammit studied martial arts under Hermann twice weekly starting in the fall of 1990, about a year before Hermann's October 31, 1991, arrest, and advanced to the orange belt level.

"I always wanted to take some kind of martial art. And Hermann was always telling Darlene that I had the kind of, well, you know, the kind of build that suited it because I was small and slim. He told me I had a good build."

A strict disciplinarian in the martial arts, Hermann found many converts to his style, according to Zammit.

"I liked the discipline. He tried to push the discipline as much as possible without turning anybody off. It was nothing too harsh. He was really trying to say to keep it [the Hapkido] for self-defence…. He always said to only use it as a last resort."

Hermann was a constant presence at the studio, occasionally darting next door to take care of his birds at Harlequin Place. "The odd time he'd step out next door. He had budgies next door, but he was always there [with us]."

One year, the annual Alliston Potato Festival featured Hermann and four of his students, including Zammit, although he admitted that "some of us were too shy to go in the parade." They marched down the main street with a banner advertising the Hapkido studio. "He had two of the younger kids holding a banner. There were about four of us behind him."

This kind of recognition helped fuel Hermann's drive to run for election to town council. The election was held after his arrest and "actually he got quite a few votes," said Zammit with a laugh. "There were a few pools going around about how many votes he'd get."

There was loyalty in Zammit's words and he told me that both he and his wife "liked Hermann a lot. We still get letters from him."

Those feeling aside, he admitted that he and others were bitter about the turn of events. "I wanted to continue with the martial arts. It kind of left me hanging in the middle. But I can't complain. He was good to us." If Zammit was short of cash for a martial arts session, Hermann would wait for the payment, preferring to continue to teach rather than hound his students for money.

Zammit was convinced that Hermann had advanced ability as a martial arts practitioner. "As far as I'm concerned, the attempted murder charges don't make sense. If he really wanted to kill somebody, he could have."

Phil, a firefighter with the Brampton Fire Department and a student at the martial arts studio who knew Hermann from 1990 to 1992, described Hermann as a disciplinarian and "a pretty good teacher. I'd say his skill was at least average. He seemed to have gone through all the paces."

The one crux? The students learned from a manual. "It was all in German, so it had to be translated." It meant that certain moves and techniques took time to learn.

But Hermann's students were a dedicated lot. Phil stuck with the lessons twice a week. Hermann was a sensible kind of guy, with "a good sense of humour and quite friendly," said Phil. "He was a little ambitious and quite anxious to get things done. He was sort of strict when it came to training."

Phil was going for his blue belt at the time of Hermann's arrest. He was not a part of the August 1991 Potato Festival Parade.

Zammit never socialized with Hermann, because of his busy schedule, but was struck most by Hermann's adherence to his martial arts. "He just figured it's good for the mind. He just couldn't understand why other people wouldn't want to do it."

Becky Smith of Bolton knew Hermann well enough to hire him on and off for a couple of years to do a variety of carpentry and renovation jobs for her. She was bright and cheerful over the phone and told me that in 1989 or 1990 she hired Hermann to do some renovation work at the fashion boutique she owned in Palgrave.

"We all liked him as a person, and he was certainly a good worker," she said. "He put a whole new front in and built some counters. And he put a deck on our home. And I never would have thought that this would happen to him. [He was] an excellent carpenter when he did the work himself. I heard from some other people whom he did work for that he was a terrific cabinet maker. He worked pretty well on and off for two years."

Becky said he was popular with the women, too. "He was always coming in and telling us about who his latest girlfriend was or whatever. He was quite a ladies' man."

She laughed. "We used to call him 'the old hippie,' because he wore his hair long pulled back in a pony tail. All the girls in the shop used to kid him about that, but he loved it.

"I just about flipped when I saw who it was who was shooting at the police. He had too much going for him. He was a very good worker when he was doing the work, and I say that because sometimes he left the men who worked for him to do the work, and they didn't do nearly as good a job. Maybe he just had too much going at once."

12

The Birdman

Budgies: Hermann loved them, and his activities as a harlequin budgie fancier linked Hermann to other breeders and exhibitors worldwide. Before his arrest, he was a Canadian correspondent for *Budgerigar World*, a British magazine catering to fanciers.

Hermann kept an extensive aviary in his farmhouse in Kleinburg. His harlequin budgies were noted for their soft and textured colour variations and were proven prize-winners.

In fact, he wrote several articles for *Budgerigar World*, including the following, devoted to his love of birds:

My Life with Birds
by Hermann Beier

For my 6th birthday, my mother gave me a wild bird as a most cherished present. Hansi filled my young life with cheerful chirping for many years until he died. Though I knew I could not replace Hansi, I missed the music of a bird around me and I missed the tranquillity of daily feeding time. I therefore bought a pair of budgies from a friend. Then, just for fun, I put a nest in the cage. A few days later my female was missing. Much to my surprise, I found her in the nest sitting on two eggs. In that first breeding she laid five eggs and hatched three chicks. I kept them all.

Later, I bought mates of the opposite sex for these budgies. I bought four additional pairs. With all of these I entered the world of bird-keeping. Then a new job opportunity resulted in a move from the city to the country, where it was finally possible to set up a much larger breeding area and flight. I then began to buy more expensive birds, became a member of a well-known West German bird club (A.Z.) and went to my first show (Provincial Show), where, to my surprise, I took second place with an Opaline Cinnamon Grey Cock.

As time went on, I was fortunate to win many more awards and medals (including Best Novice in the West German National Show in 1976 with a yellowface cobalt cock). Meanwhile, a fascination and love of recessive pieds was developing. I bought a pair split for recessive pied. These were the beginning of all my future recessive pieds, which later won awards throughout West Germany.

My decision to come to Canada in 1980 meant that I had to sell all of my beloved birds. This was perhaps my greatest heartbreak. However, in less than four years I had built up a new aviary with about a hundred birds. My recessive pieds are among the best in my new country. The sounds of birds fill my life with joy, happiness, and tranquillity once again. My life is centred around birds and my birds are around me.

Hermann's sisters would no doubt agree.

Renate Schlottmann of Mississauga was the oldest of Hermann's three sisters (one other, Helga, was also living in Canada; a third sister, Elli, lived in Germany). Renate told me that when the family moved from East to West Germany in 1945, they had virtually nothing. But despite a tough life at the beginning, the situation stabilized after their father joined them after his war service ended.

"Father was an officer in a jail and wanted Hermann to be a police officer," she told me over the telephone. "All the men [at the time] like it that way [for their sons], that they go the same way they do."

As a young man, Hermann excelled at sports and in his schoolwork in the small city of Hamm. He also developed a keen interest in animals.

"Hermann has always liked animals," said his sister. "He was always having fish or other things. And then he tried with the birds."

When details of his exploits came to light, Hermann found himself enjoying a celebrity that was far-reaching in the bird world.

The January 1992 issue of *Budgerigar World* ran an editorial under its "B.W. Correspondents" banner:

> *Budgerigar World* readers of long standing will know that our list of Foreign Correspondents, whilst remaining fairly stable, have seen the changes over the past nine years. A few fanciers, such as Ole Gade from Denmark, have been with us since day one, whilst others are recently additions or changes to the list.
>
> Many of our past Correspondents are still active within the hobby, others not, but none have presented me with the surprise that I had when reading the *Toronto Star* recently. Here was a photograph of Hermann

Beier, former Canadian Correspondent to *B.W.* and the headline read, "Breeder of Budgies Charged After Chase." It appears that Beier now faces numerous robbery and weapons charges and a charge of attempted murder, after police from four jurisdictions were led on a wild, high-speed car chase over 75 miles of winding rural roads.

Kellie Hudson of the newspaper reported that "The man exchanged gunfire with officers throughout the 45-minute chase, firing at them from crests of hills and shooting at a police helicopter." The chase happened after he'd allegedly robbed three banks in under an hour armed with a sawed-off shotgun, smoke bombs and other weapons.

There surely must be an easier way to raise the cash for that outcross. [*Outcross* is a term for a bird — often an expensive one — which adds new genetic material to a breeder's stock to rid it of undesirable traits.]

Budgerigar World's gaff did not go unnoticed. Tom Knox (referred to in the publication only as Tom Knox, Canada) wrote to the editor in March 1992:

> Sir.
>
> Having read your Editorial in the January 1992 issue of *BW*, I am of the opinion the "Breeder of Budgies Charged After Chase" should never have appeared. Sensational journalism should be left to the tabloids and not the Fancy [budgie breeders] Press.
>
> The motive of the Canadian person who supplied the article escapes me. They would have been better giving some understanding and sympathy to the situation. This article should never have left Canada.

Budgerigar World's reply was terse:

I can only apologise for any upset that my editorial reference in connection with this subject has caused to the Canadian Fancy. The material was given to me by a person whom I was assured was the representative of the Canadian B.S. [Budgie Society]. I have since learnt that the Canadian B.S. is not the National Body.

This didn't say much for the sensitivity of *Budgerigar World*. Hermann's civil lawyers, Paula Beard and James Carlisle, took exception to the magazine's treatment of their client. They spoke to me about it in late 1993. After the editorial was brought to their attention, they dispatched a letter to *Budgerigar World* in January 1993:

Although it is true that certain allegations have been made against Mr. Beier, he was embarrassed and upset that these allegations should be repeated in your magazine. Mr. Beier is a respected breeder of budgerigar with a worldwide reputation. Your magazine is read by budgerigar fanciers throughout the world and is a proper for [*sic*] organ for disseminating the information for the care and breeding of these birds. However, there is no justification for spreading gossip concerning charges against any person when those charges have no relation to the care and breeding of budgerigars.

You have besmirched Mr. Beier's reputation throughout the community of Budgerigar fanciers without any justification.

On Mr. Beier's behalf, I demand an apology for the damage you have done to his good name throughout the Budgerigar world. If such an apology is forthcoming Mr. Beier may decide to take no further action.

I await your prompt reply.

Paula Beard said it was clear that a response was necessary.

The magazine had published "what they thought was probably an amusing little item," she said, adding that it brought an issue that was originally confined to Canada onto the world scene. "It went on to talk about — in quite scandalous terms — the legal difficulty Hermann was having. There is no reason for people outside Ontario and certainly not outside Canada to really know about this episode in Hermann's life. So, he was quite upset and he asked us to complain to them. We sent them a letter and we got back a rather nice apology.

"Within a week the editor phoned me and the upshot of which is this letter [of apology] which he sent and one of the concerns [he expressed] was that if they printed up something in the editorial, something apologizing again, now, more than a year later, wouldn't it just bring it up in the public eye again, who by now would have forgotten it? We said we would ask Hermann whether the apology was sufficient or whether he wanted something written in the paper. Hermann seemed satisfied with the written apology he got back, so we didn't ask them to run another editorial and we didn't sue them."

Hermann's escapade didn't escape the notice of another writer whose stock in trade is humour. On February 7, 1993, the *Toronto Star* ran a column by award-winning humour columnist Joey Slinger under the headline "Beware — Budgie Breeding Can Drive You Berserk." In it he refers to "a budgie breeder gone wig city":

> I keep a close watch for news of budgie breeders (this might be an appropriate moment to introduce an International Haywire Budgie Breeder Alert) because I was once a budgie breeder and ran into troubles myself. This particular budgie breeder has pleaded guilty to robbing eight banks and a credit union and attempting to murder 13 police officers and endangering the lives of nine other police officers by either shooting at them or aiming of three pistols he carried at them during and after a 97-mile-an-hour chase that started in Guelph (curiously, that is where my budgie-breeding difficulties started, too) and ended when he crashed his stolen stretch limousine, its right front tire shot out, into a ditch. The budgie breeder ended up with bullet wounds in the hip, the abdomen and both calves.

My troubles never amounted to anything like that. But they did leave emotional scars that still carry. I don't know whether his experience or mine is the more common, but I know that everyone who starts out hoping to make the big time on the proceeds of budgie breeding sees their plans come to grief.

The problem lies in telling one budgie from another, gender-wise. It is something budgies know, I presume, but it is a mystery to everyone else, and even if you teach your budgies to talk they won't help you out. "Who's a pretty boy know," is a pretty evasive answer, when you get right down to it. Anyway, if you get it wrong, you will have nothing to show for your budgie breeding efforts but a seething frustration.

Witness the budgie breeder who turned into a one-person Bonnie and Clyde ...

The column continued for a few more lines, finishing with Slinger breathing a literary sigh of relief that he got out of budgie breeding when he did — "at age eight."

Curiously enough, Slinger was later approached by the Budgerigar and Foreign Bird Society; its officials liked his column and, apparently not feeling too kindly about the memory of Hermann Beier, asked Slinger to hand out championship trophies at an upcoming show.

Did he do it? I sought out Slinger, whose whereabouts at the *Toronto Star* were, according to an item in the satire magazine *Frank*, suspect at best; he was working some days at the Book Cellar book store in Toronto's high-class Yorkville area while recharging his creative batteries, and that was where I found him.

I contacted him on a hot weekday afternoon in midsummer. He was pulled to the phone, away from his book-shelving duties. Pleasant but guarded, he didn't want to talk about Hermann Beier. "That was just the subject of one of my columns. But it's a very interesting story."

He confirmed that he was approached by Hermann's old club to act as an official at a bird club event. He had declined: "I didn't know how serious the offer was."

He offered me a quick "good luck with the book," before hanging up.

For budgie aficionados, their greatest energies are focused on their birds. At a show for young budgies and cockatiels in May 1993, I asked a member of the Budgerigar and Foreign Bird Society to comment on Hermann's situation. Insiders said that several members of the club had turned their backs on Hermann, deserting him when he needed their support.

The show was being held at the Banbury Community Centre, a big, airy recreation hall set amid birch and maple trees in the upscale Lawrence Avenue East–Leslie Street area of Don Mills. A row of short evergreens lined a flagstone walkway leading from the parking lot to the front door. Scruffy brown sparrows, seedy cousins to the elite prizewinners inside, scratched about in the dirt at the base of the trees, taking dust baths.

I found a member of the club who was willing to chat. Now, this man — I'll call him Bill — couldn't possibly strike anyone as the kind who would wish ill upon anybody. About six feet tall, a little stooped, he had a friendly, deeply creased face, the wrinkles turning into major fissures when he smiled, spreading up and around this tanned, leathery map and joining other fissures to form deeper folds.

All Bill really wanted to talk about was his cockatiels. "I've raised some of the best in Canada, you know," he said, nodding. One learns quickly that in the bird world you have to be a good self-promoter; it's no good to be shy. And so bird folk have no pretensions when it comes to crowing about their birds.

But enough about birds. "What about Hermann?" I asked him.

"He's in jail," Bill said, with just a hint of a grin. "He ran into a bit of trouble. He was the president of the club at one time, you know."

He moved down a row of cages, many adorned with ribbons. Bill's attention was riveted on his birds. He was obviously proud of them, the way Hermann had been, the way most of the top breeders are. Cockatiels were Bill's specialty, but he also bred parrots.

In another room, people relaxed in lawn chairs in front of a bank of cages; three cages high, they were arranged like a set of television monitors placed one on top of another. All that was missing was the gentle blue glow. Inside, the budgies bobbed and chuckled and tweeted and made sounds like cellophane crinkling and Christmas bells tinkling, hopping from one perch to the other and back again. The human faces were rapt, attentive, absorbed; the bird faces were comical, ringed in blue and green and mauve and yellow; they bounced about like clowns performing for a silently appreciative audience.

If you love birds, you're serious about it.

"Now look at the chest on that one." Bill gestured to a young bird of a colour referred to by breeders as *opaline*. Its soft grey feathers carried a lilac sheen, as if lightly shellacked with a purplish glaze. "See that chest? It's full. It's strong, not skinny. That's going to be a prize-winner when he's older. And you see how his wing tips just meet across the back? That's the way the wings should be. You take a look at all of these winners, and I've either bred them or my birds have been involved somehow."

George Pappas bred English show budgies, the kind Hermann specialized in, called recessive pieds or harlequins. He met Hermann in 1985 through other breeders. At the time he was living in Marathon, Ontario; when I spoke with him, he had retired from his job as a teacher and principal and was living in Warsaw, a village just outside Peterborough.

His interest in harlequin budgies had led him to Hermann and he talked about him warmly. "He sent me a lovely pair of these budgies all the way to Marathon and at only half the price of what would normally be charged. Through the years, between 1985 and 1990, when I was teaching school up there, I would drop down on March Break. I'd visit him and buy a couple of birds from him.

"Every time I visited him [his birds] were very well taken care of. In his dealing with me personally, I always found him very friendly, very helpful, and he always gave me a very decent price on birds. We both wanted to keep the rarer budgie colours going. It's difficult to enter shows with them. Because they're recessive, the birds tend to be smaller than others."

That means they're less robust and more prone to infections. They die more easily. And so they attract less interest among fanciers (and judges) who tend to approach their hobby with a Darwinian desire for absolute, resolute toughness and mettle. Birds just *have to* survive. But with a you and me against the world attitude that the recessive pied breeders share, "we both worked toward making sure there were adequate awards for these [recessive pied] birds."

Colour-wise, a recessive pied, Pappas explained, is like a pinto horse; the lower breast can be any one of the following colours: light green, sky blue, violet, cobalt, or mauve, which contrasts with the upper portions of the bird. There are also patches of one of the following: black or combinations of green/yellow/black, blue/white/black, or violet. Cobalt blue is one of the rarest. "These ones rarely win in shows," said Pappas, somewhat sadly.

Like all good teachers, Pappas, who joined the Budgerigar and Foreign Bird Society in 1991, and kept between two and three hundred birds at a time himself, was a great source of information. He told me budgie breeding was strongest in England, where you might find anywhere from six to seven thousand birds at a show. Germany, Belgium, France, Austria, and the Scandinavian countries also had strong budgie contingents.

According to the *Encyclopedia of Cage and Aviary Birds* by Cyril H. Rogers, in the early twentieth century, recessive pied characteristics showed up in shipments of green budgies throughout Europe, in which the birds had "a few yellow feathers on back of head, tail, or wings."

They were considered "mismarked," and were frowned upon by fanciers. That changed in the 1930s. In Denmark in 1933, green and yellow pied mutations occurred among a mixed colony of budgies. Herr C. af Enchjelm, curator of the Helsinki Zoological Gardens, recognized their significance and began developing a blue and white strain of the bird. In 1948, Rogers received several birds and founded "the first Recessive Pied strain in Britain [by this time it was known that the Danish breed of pieds was recessive and could be bred in all colour forms]."

Pappas said Hermann's birds were high quality. An individual from good stock would cost about $250. He told me his relationship with Hermann was strictly confined to birds. "I would talk to him occasionally or see him at a show," said Pappas. "We didn't socialize."

Proving once again that it's a very small world indeed, an ambulance attendant who took Hermann to hospital the day he was shot by police just happened to be a member of the society, according to Pappas. Afterward, the news spread through the budgie world like a flock of harlequins let loose.

"It took me five phone calls to find out where he was," said Pappas, although he admitted to having spoken to him only a couple of times since the arrest. He quickly added, however, that Hermann made a very unselfish act of donating all of his trophies (about thirty, Pappas estimates) to the society to be used in subsequent shows.

§

In the early 1980s, a fellow budgie enthusiast, Jenny, had met Hermann through her bird fancier clubs.

The two became friends, meeting in cities across the province and in the United States at club functions. Their approach to bird breeding was different — Jenny focused strongly on her four-thousand-strong flock; Hermann, with only about 5 percent of her number, concentrated on importing harlequins from overseas.

The robberies were "so out of character for those of us who knew him," said Jenny. She believed him to be engaged to an American woman. "He was engaged to a girl from the States who was a bird judge. I think he might have gone off the deep end, to put it quite bluntly. Right after Halloween, I went to a bird show in Detroit and ran into her [Hermann's fiancée] and asked if she had heard, and she had. It was his age, too. Something happened to make him snap."

Jenny told me they kept in touch and that he called her periodically.

Perhaps the most touching tribute to Hermann came from Kathleen, a chemist in her early thirties and a fellow member of the bird club. Hermann considered her a protégé, someone to whom he offered fatherly advice and guidance.

I met Kathleen at a restaurant near the laboratory where she worked. Kathleen was quiet and shy; she lived with her parents in a solidly middle class neighbourhood in the then-suburb of North York, now north-central Toronto. It didn't surprise me that her home and place of work were only a few kilometres away from each other. She struck me as someone who thrived on a sense of order, peace, and quiet.

She ordered a Bloody Caesar and sipped on it through a little red straw as she explained how she met Hermann at a bird show and only got to know him because her mother and Hermann, both German, had struck up a conversation. Kathleen herself didn't speak German.

All of the events surrounding Hermann's arrest came as a shock to her. From the chase to the shootout to the court case, it all disturbed her.

There were two groups of supporters of Hermann — those who have defended him and those who would like to make a mockery of him, she said. She was avowedly in the former group, she stressed.

She kept in touch with Hermann, and received regular collect phone calls from him. She never visited him in prison, though. The thought of having to go through the interrogation procedures for a visit, of having the details of your life examined by a government agency, "just to gain access to see a friend," bothered her. I was hard-pressed to think of anything that this person might want to hide.

I asked her what she thought happened to all the money he took. After all, he couldn't have spent all of it, could he?

"Why do you want to find out so much about Hermann?" she asked. "Besides, why can't he have the money? He's got to have something to spend when he gets out, doesn't he?"

I didn't bother to remind her that it wasn't his money in the first place, and changed the subject. I was curious about what their relationship had been like. I asked her point-blank if she had ever been romantically involved with Hermann, despite their age difference of twenty-plus years. It seemed reasonable to me that they might have been involved, given that she fit the personality type to which Hermann was attracted: a little shy and unassertive.

"No," she told me as she sipped her drink. It was a pretty clear that *no* implied that there were no sparks; perhaps she saw him as a father figure.

After their initial meeting, Kathleen got to know Hermann quite well. He provided her with some budgie pairs as she became more interested in birds; he also did some bird-sitting when her family went away on vacation. Because of Hermann, Kathleen became more involved in the club and eventually served as secretary-treasurer and later as a director.

Kathleen passed me some photographs across the sticky tabletop: there was a picture of her receiving a trophy from a grey-jacketed man with a moustache. She is out of focus in the picture, but off to the left, looking like a squinting Popeye, a grinning, muscle-shirted Hermann, bulging forearms crossed, surveys the scene like a proud papa or a smiling, benevolent teacher.

Another is of Hermann's businesses in Alliston, three in a row at the little plaza: Hermann's gym, Harlequin Place, and the never-to-be-opened Hermann's Pool & Darts Hall. Two others are of Hermann's birds: aviaries of chicken wire with wood slats for the birds to perch on, the floors covered in newspaper, and rows of green and blue and yellow budgies sitting under the bright fluorescent light glowing in the upper reaches.

She then showed me another trophy shot: in it, Kathleen, dressed in blue jeans and a sweatshirt decorated with parrots and emblazoned with Toronto Parrot Club, stands awkwardly at a fold-out table littered with pop tins and budgie trophies. Around her neck are several winning medallions hanging on red, white, and blue ribbons. Her mother, framed by an arch of gold budgie trophies, looks on. Also in the photo, half turning toward the camera, is Hermann. He is wearing a white shirt and black vest and sporting a neatly trimmed moustache.

During Hermann's trial and in response to a request from Hermann's lawyer, Paul Stern, Kathleen wrote the following letter to Justice Kenneth Langdon in support of her friend. Here is an excerpt:

Mr. Justice K. Langdon

Dear Sir:
I am a friend of Hermann Beier. I am … Canadian-born and university-educated with a Bachelor of Science…. I am currently working as an analytical technician. I am also a breeder and exhibitor of Budgerigars and Parrotlets. I am a member of several bird clubs throughout the world as well as the Budgerigar and Foreign Bird Society of Canada in Toronto, which is where I met Hermann Beier.

I met him one day at a bird show in Toronto and I met him through my mother. Since he is German, my mother heard his accent, since she is German, and started speaking to him. Since I am the bird breeder in the family she introduced him to me. He was a very easy person to meet because of his friendly nature and good manners. My father being an Englishman found no problem talking with him either. Since he is a Champion breeder and a budgerigar judge, a very high and respected position, and I am only a Novice breeder, he was very helpful to me and to other breeders.

I have known him for several years, perhaps 7 or 8 years. He has always been very friendly, polite and considerate. One year when my family was going on vacation he looked after my birds while we were away. We were very grateful that he did this for us as not many people would want to look after the 40 birds that I had. He had a very nice house and a very clean bird room. Since he is an animal lover, he made a very nice place for his birds and his dogs.

Years later, in 1989–1990, he became the president of the Budgerigar and Foreign Bird Society of Canada. Previous years he had been the Show manager. He did his best in both position [*sic*] his only problem was his English as he could not always make his thoughts known. That same year I had become Secretary of the club. Through being secretary I got to know more about him. He had his own business, Hermann the Handyman, as well as a Martial Arts and Fitness School. He was very busy and hardworking person. The craftsmanship of his aviary showed professionalism and a lot of hard work he put in. He was always trying to make things work the best they could and even under pressure he was still polite and calm. He is a very talkative person and always bubbling full of laughter and energy.

In my opinion he was trying to do too many things, too much work and in the small town where he lived and worked, so the more he tried to expand his business the more money he needed and unfortunately not enough customers to make ends meet and with unsuccessful bank loans he had no other way of getting money so out of a few acts of desperation he turned to crime.

Everyone who knew him did not believe it. It was a hard thing to believe. When I first heard about it through someone, I thought it was a joke, but it was no joke to see his picture in the newspaper and get a phone call from his sister. It was completely out of character for him to do something like that.

He was and still is an honest person and if it wasn't for his hardships and also the break-up of him and his fiancée, then he would not be in this situation. But I believe that he has learned his lesson the hard way and he will not repeat his mistake of turning to crime to solve his problems.

He is now like the bird in the cage which is waiting for freedom. So I do not think he would risk his freedom again to be put back in the cage by doing anything wrong again. I know he will have the support of his friends and family when he gets out because we all miss him at the bird club.

Hermann Beier is my friend and everyone's so I hope his sentence is not so heavy since he is a good-hearted and good-natured person.

Yours truly,
Kathleen B.

In a later telephone conversation, Kathleen told me she missed Hermann, but enjoyed receiving letters from him decorated with his art.

"He really is an excellent artist," she said. "He should get in touch with Hallmark [the greeting card company]. He can do that sort of thing from prison, can't he? After all, the Birdman of Alcatraz wrote a book."

13

Collins Bay Penitentiary

THE INMATES, AND JUST ABOUT EVERYBODY ELSE WHO IS FAMILIAR WITH it, refer to Collins Bay Penitentiary as "Disneyland" because of its pitched red roof. A pleasant sweep of red tile perches over a front door that looks as if it should lead to a wonderland of fun. That is, until you see the walls — six metres high, rims topped by barbed wire and very serious-looking razor-wire curlicues that twist and turn above it. The thick brick walls seem to go on forever, stretching out on either side of the entrance. The building, which opened in 1930, was not meant to be broken out of.

Hermann's old home at Millhaven, by contrast, opened in 1971. Unlike Collins Bay, it's a maximum security facility that houses about 400 inmates, compared to Disneyland's 492. While it has a permanent inmate population, Millhaven is primarily what is known as a "receiving institution," a stopover for inmates on their way to other institutions.

But Collins Bay evokes a sense of permanence that begins at its walls. Though formidable, it's classed as a medium security institution. Maximum security is defined as being necessary for inmates who are considered to make active efforts to escape custody and, if they escape, are considered dangerous. As a result, a maximum institution has tight perimeter security and restricted movement through the facility. Medium security is for inmates who are not considered to be an active threat to escape. There is tight perimeter security, but movement within is less restricted.

Collins Bay Penitentiary is often called Disneyland for its colourful, castle-like façade. Inside, though, it's no picnic. But Hermann found romance and marriage within its walls.

During times of disruption, a prison is put into a "lockdown" situation. If information is received that there are problems, all inmates are returned to their cells, where they are kept until the situation is under control.

When I arrived at Collins Bay to interview Hermann in October 1993, I entered through a set of glass doors that led to yet another big sliding glass door that was operated electronically by a guard. The front lobby sported walls of speckled yellowy composite stone like those found in public schools built in the 1960s. It was here that I first picked up the odour of alcohol — it didn't smell like disinfectant alcohol, either, but straight-to-the-gut, let's-line-dance rye whisky. I found that strange.

The reception area was cordoned off from the building on either side by electronically controlled barred doors that, with just a touch of whimsy, were comprised of curving, S-shaped pieces of metal painted a flat yellow.

But at that point I was more concerned about just getting in. I passed through a doorway-frame metal detector and a guard's voice strained through a little window in a smoked-glass enclosure, asking me what I wanted.

"Okay," the voice said, after I explained the reason for my visit. I could just make out a figure through the smoky glass. There was much flipping of paper on a clipboard, and then the voice said, "There's no record of you here to visit."

I reeled off the names of the people I spoke with in order to get in — senior staffers at the prison, the unit manager at the prison, Hermann's social worker — and was finally cleared to enter after a few pleasant-sounding by unpleasantly direct questions:

"Are you a friend?"

"No, I'm writing a story about Mr. Beier."

"Are you a friend?" (They clearly didn't like the "Mister" stuff. As at other institutions, the guards refer to inmates by their surnames only.)

"No."

The guard turned toward someone inside the office and said, "This guy's here to see Beier."

"Go get Beier, please," I heard another voice say.

The rules: no camera, two pieces of I.D. only, no more than six dollars in your pocket, and nothing else.

I put my stuff in a locker in another room and moved to my right as instructed. Here I waited until a set of doors opened. After they had closed behind me, I proceeded through to the visitor's lounge. A woman who was opening some mail smiled and said hello to me, laying down her letter-opener for a moment as if to begin a conversation. But instead she reached for a telephone.

A man in a booth with panels of lights and buttons, the person controlling access to the visitor's lounge, went through the same motions as the first guard. He looked to be about twenty-four, with a thick moustache and heavy eyes. "Are you a friend? You're not on the list," he said.

I gave him the same names as before, the officials who clearly had rank. He admitted my legitimacy to be here, but wheezed, "Jeez, they should have put you in the list."

I was finally given entry to the lounge, a large open room carpeted with a rust-coloured, indoor-outdoor rug. Square wooden tables were scattered around the room, the centres of which were raised about two inches above the rest of the table, I assumed for greater visibility by the guards in case visitors and inmates tried to pass items back and forth.

The table I sat down at had I LOVE MICHELLE BROWN carved into it.

Six couples sat talking; they were mostly young, in their early twenties. There was one African-Canadian couple who never took their eyes off each other; the rest were white, with tattoos and long stringy hair — the men had an "Axl Rose" look to them; their women, heavily made up and pouty-lipped, seemed to stare blankly at nothing in particular. There's a lot of emptiness here, time that needs to be filled in a contrived way. How do you open up in a place like this? Who would want to? The black couple looked as if they were straining to create a sense of intimacy in a place where intimacy was forbidden.

The most heavy-metal-looking of the inmates got up and went to the guard station. He passed his I.D. through the window and received a cribbage board. There was an inky blue-green dagger on his forearm, which was devoid of hair, thin and strangely smooth and feminine-looking.

But my observations were cut short as I was called back to the guard station. "You aren't supposed to be here," I was told accusingly. "You're supposed to have an interview room."

I was told to come back out, and then was instructed, via an intercom, to go through a particular set of steel-barred doors. The guard motioned to the doors. "Go through there," he told me. The first set of bars was opened for me electronically, sliding across the concrete floor with the heavy metallic *click-ka-chunk* that is a familiar sound in prisons. I stepped through the open door and saw a second set of locked steel bars. The first door closed, and I was stuck in this passageway. I waited and waited for the second set of steel bars to open, restricted to a space about six feet wide and eight feet long, a corridor between the front section of the prison, outside of the lounge area but still within the confines of the institution proper, and the interview area. I stared at the guard through the window of the office with a look in my eyes that said, *So, are you going to let me through?* But he ignored me. He knew I was there, but for some unknown reason he kept me waiting for almost fifteen minutes while he leafed through a magazine. And again I wondered, as I had at Millhaven, whether this was some kind of a joke, some sort of cruel gag meant to make me feel uncertain, trapped, claustrophobic.

At last, the second door slid open. Another guard ushered me past the guard station to the hallway that led to the interview rooms, located off to the side of the corridor. Hermann was already there waiting for me, smiling and looking relaxed. He was even joking with the guards. As he greeted me, I noticed he had lost some weight. He had also grown a beard, silvery and sharp. Two crucifixes, silver and wood, dangled from his neck.

Together, we continued down the narrow corridor and into a four-by-five metre, high-ceilinged room that was painted a pale blue. We sat down across from each other at a plain wooden table. Through a window that opened onto an enclosed courtyard I could see a maintenance truck sitting unattended. Although the room was warm, the open window permitted a cool breeze into the room. Every once in a while, the breeze would pick up, giving me intermittent chills throughout our conversation.

Hermann said his appeal process was continuing. He claimed that his lawyer, Paul Stern, was angry about the results of the court action — too much prison time given the circumstances — and so he had promised to get Hermann "the best lawyer he could find."

That lawyer was Brian Greenspan.

Hermann was still seething over the allegations connecting him with the robberies in the Lake Simcoe area in July, 1991. "I wasn't there. This is wrong. They [the authorities] say, 'there were robberies there? Maybe it was Hermann.'"

He then moved on to other topics, such as his health and the routine at the prison. Hermann was waiting to have surgery done on his hip. "I walk around and I get this squeaky sound, it is squeaking," he told me. He also needed to have a procedure done on his knee, which had nothing to do with the injuries suffered during his arrest, but which had given him ongoing problems going back thirty years.

Hermann's daily routine at Collins Bay would begin at 7:00 a.m. with breakfast. At 8:00 he would start work. "Here you get a few dollars a day, six dollars a day. That is the money you can spend in the canteen." At 11:30 there was a break for lunch, unless, as in Hermann's case, there was work to be done on specific projects, such as a prison-based furniture company initiative of which he was a part (in that case, lunch would be delayed until 1:00 p.m.). At noon was the count, and everybody had to be accounted for; then more work until 3:45 p.m. There was another count after that, then dinner. The evening was spent however the inmate decided.

In the evenings, Hermann would busy himself with a wood burning set or writing and drawing at his desk, for which he built an extension to hold all of his materials. His artwork was simple but colourful. Birds drawn from nature books — terns, chickadees, and doves — as well as crucifixes and flowers decorated the left side of the envelopes in which he placed his letters. He also took long walks in the exercise yard, usually alone, but sometimes with one of the two or three inmates he considered friends.

The anger was starting to subside. "I control myself more," he told me. He also mentioned that Collins Bay had agreed to hire a professional teacher to lead the anger management group that Hermann had started at Millhaven. He had led the group there, but said that acceptance of an inmate-led group would not be as well-received by inmates at Collins Bay.

14

REHABILITATION

ANGER MANAGEMENT IS WHAT INTERESTED HERMANN THE MOST; FOR OTHers, there were groups that assisted inmates to get over their drug and alcohol dependencies. But there was nothing that truly addressed rehabilitation as it related to getting along in the world outside the penitentiary, Hermann said. "What they have in terms of rehabilitation, there's nothing. They put a notice on the bulletin board and the inmates are walking by and [the attitude toward it is] nothing. They don't teach you about life on the outside."

He claimed other inmates came to him to talk. "An inmate I don't know, he said 'Can I walk with you? I want to ask you something.' Most of them are younger. And they say 'Hermann, I don't know what happened, I'm fed up with the system. Teach me how to live a life outside. Teach me how the life [is to be lived] outside.' These people get out on the streets and they can't handle it and they do something so they can get back in. They have a room, they have food, and they have a roof over their heads. But they say to me 'I want to have a life, I want to have a family.'"

Hermann whirled his hands around, rotating them over and under each other to emphasis the point, then slammed them, palms down, on the wooden table. A large mosquito that had somehow survived the cool fall weather was humming about the room. It drifted with the breeze over the interview table; seemingly without a thought, Hermann commandingly snapped his palms together, sandwiching it in midair, crushing it, then wiping the remains from his hands. Bits of mosquito fell to the floor.

Hermann was plenty ticked about drugs, too, and people making their own hooch from various foods and sugar. Drugs got into the institution very easily, he told me. "I don't know so much, but it's easy." Granted, there may have been extenuating circumstances when I was there, but at the time I could confirm this myself — I was never frisked, never even closely checked. No guard came within five feet of me. And in the interview room, no one could have seen drugs being passed under the table if that had been my intention. "The drugs [and drug abuse] go [on] in here," said Hermann. "And it's a terrible thing because I am still so against drugs." He said that in the prison "it's a big business, selling and dealing in drugs. It's incredible. You see guys walking high around here."

This reminded me of the case of Canadian boxing legend George Chuvalo's son, Georgie Lee, who spent time at Collins Bay and Warkworth penitentiaries for armed robbery. He couldn't escape his drug addiction, and his life ended when he injected himself with near-pure heroin in a dingy Toronto hotel room. Two of Chuvalo's other sons also suffered from, and died as a result of, drug addiction.

Hermann re-emphasized his positive relationship with the guards and his easy-going rapport with them: "I am respectful of them and they are respectful of me. When I ask sometimes I get what I want because they know I am not using them."

I didn't get a chance to see Hermann's "house," his cell, which he said was the standard size, about eight by ten feet and nine feet high, but he was undeniably proud of it. "I have shelves and art books and my private clothes, which I cannot wear now [because of the interview — any time outside of their houses, inmates must wear prison-issue blue jeans and red golf-shirt]. I don't see any problems where I am in the block. It is all lifers in the block where I am." Their relative age (most were "a little older" than other inmates, Hermann said carefully) helped because they tended to be less rowdy. His cell had a solid door with one small window at eye level; it effectively blocked out the noise when it was closed, making the inside of the cell quite peaceful. This was something he appreciated.

Hermann had seen three lockdowns since his arrival. Anytime there was a disruption, such as a violent fight, the inmates were locked in their cells for a period of time, during which there was an investigation. The most recent lockdown had lasted four days. There was some "heat between blacks and whites," he said, referring to the heightened racial tension at the facility. "That means we're sitting four days in our cells, we can't go anywhere ..." Food was served to the prisoners in their cells: "So, I say [jokingly], 'finally we get room service!'"

Hermann had never been in the "hole" or solitary confinement at Collins Bay, although there was an incident with a cuff key at Metro West Detention Centre — he declined to go into any detail — after which he was placed in the hole at that location. "I try not to give the guards or the institution a reason," he said.

The only minor dispute that concerned him at that time was a gift of coloured pencils and markers that he had received from a female friend, a minister with a Christian open-church sect with whom he exchanged letters. He was still waiting to be allowed to have the materials to use for his artwork: "I am tired after [waiting] two months already. I can buy markers ... just blue or ... red, green, or black [but] I want to have *all* the colours."

Smack! His hand came down hard on another hapless mosquito. He continued: "This woman friend, we get to know each other through other inmates."

15

A New Calling

Hermann looked up, wiped what remained of the mosquito from his hands, and smiled. His next words came as quite a surprise to me: "I have become a minister now, too." His rekindled interest in religion led him to look into ways to strengthen his commitment to God. This revelation marked the end of our first visit at Collin's Bay. I was advised by a guard that our time was up; Hermann embraced me, and then he went one way — back to his unit — and I went the other.

Once back outside, I took a moment to admire the Disney-fied look of the place one more time before I drove away.

Hermann confirmed his new ministerial status in a letter a few days later: "Last Wednesday, October 20, 1993 ... I received my valid Minister card, certificate will follows [sic] and [you] can call me now Pastor and Rev. Also I will receive in the near future another Ministry certificate and can ministry [sic] everywhere in North America. I let you know. Please forgive me if I say that, next letters please write to 'Rev. Hermann Beier.'"

He also asked that the words *Collins Bay* be omitted from the address, indicating that the P.O. number was enough. "Now I can [begin] officially helping people," he wrote. "But first I have to talk to higher Authorities here." He ended the letter with "God bless you. I will pray for you. Hermann Beier, Rev." There was an arrow after this that pointed to the next page, where he had added "Have already a name for my Ministry but I will wait until I receive all papers etc. H."

On the outside of the envelope was a drawing of a dove with an olive branch over the words PEACE AND LOVE written in block letters. So, the next letter I wrote to him, I addressed to: Rev. Hermann Beier, P.O. Box 6700, Kingston, Ontario.

In a later letter, Hermann told me the names of two of the churches at which he had become a minister: the Universal Life Church and the American Fellowship Church (he said there was also a third for which he was still awaiting paperwork). A trip to the reference library and the retrieval of the hefty *Encyclopedia of American Religions, 3rd Edition*, provided some answers.

Based in Modesto, California, the Universal Life Church was founded by Kirby J. Hensley, an illiterate Baptist minister from North Carolina. Self-educated and influenced by his study of world religion, he hit upon an idea of a universal church that would be a unifying, rather than a divisive, force.

Hensley opened a "garage church," which in 1962 became the Universal Life Church. In order to give increasing numbers of converts access to expression, he began to ordain ministers for free, regardless of their personal beliefs. Upon request, a one-page information sheet plus an ordination certificate were presented to the new minister. The church reported in 1988 to have 12 million followers worldwide and more than 2,500 churches.

Hensley's popularity spread throughout the late 1960s, thanks to extensive media coverage and his penchant for committing outrageous acts, such as addressing large college classes and ordaining the entire audience on the spot. Ordination was free, but for twenty dollars a customer could receive a Doctorate of Divinity with ten how-to lessons on establishing and operating a church. When Hensley ran into trouble for issuing degrees from an unaccredited institution in California, he moved his education department to Phoenix, Arizona.

The doctrine of the Universal Life Church is as follows: You make up your own. None is established, though Hensley developed a personal (and varied) theology encompassing the following beliefs: reincarnation; Jesus as a being more intelligent than most men; God is substance manifest in natural laws; the soul is the continuing essence of man; heaven is having what you want; hell is a lack of what you want. For Hensley, the separation of church and state came two thousand years before the Great Flood, beginning six thousand years of spiritual dispensation, ending in thirty years of turmoil around 2000 A.D., resulting in the church and state reuniting under the banner of Universal Life. There's no record of this happening.

Hensley had run for governor of California and president of the United States under the People's Peace Prosperity Party, and his "reforms" included marrying a couple in a trial marriage and, at the 1971 Universal Life Church, "marrying two girls," the *Encyclopedia of American Religions* states.

The church ran the Universal Life Church Press Association. By 1974 it had churches and ministers in almost every state and abroad; it also held an annual convention. Hensley claimed to have ordained more than six million ministers by 1977, with 25,000 of them having formed congregations that met in small groups at house churches.

The one big problem the church faced was that it had been seen as a tax-dodge by the Internal Revenue Service, with ministers and their congregations carefully scrutinized, with occasional charges levelled of profit-making ventures being carried out under the taxation safety net of a church. The church had in turn fielded suits against the IRS to attempt to overturn denials of state-tax exemption and to gain recognition for its ministers to perform marriages. This led to many congregations seeking their own charters, effectively separating themselves from the Universal Life Church.

And then there was Hermann's other ministry, the American Fellowship Church of Rolling Bay, Washington. It was formed in 1975 by T.H. Swenson as an independent church believing in individual responsibility for spiritual growth and development. Originally called the Mother Earth Church, it described itself as a "church without walls," with widely scattered membership; no matter where they were, ministers united daily in prayer and meditation at 7:00 a.m. and 7:00 p.m. (Pacific Standard Time). There was an International Clergy Association open to ordained ministers only. There was no report of membership numbers, although the group did publish a newsletter.

It was all very striking, this notion of a church where you could become a minister just by *being*. It offered Hermann an opportunity to feel that he was doing well, to really believe that he was delivering the message of God. And to gather up all of the power and respect that went with it.

Maybe a member of the First Nations community said it best. I listened to a speech in the fall of 1993 by writer Basil Johnston, an Anishinaabe and member of the Chippewas of Nawash Unceded First Nation. Johnston pointed out that different perceptions are a mainstay of Native culture, centred on an ideal of fully appreciating the inherent goodness of life. The word *Anishnawbek* means "the Good Beings."

"People mean well; they intend well. People start out with the best of intentions, but sometimes they have to be helped back to the right path. That is how we understand human nature," Johnston said, adding that in the Anishinaabe language, the meaning of truth is "he is right, she is right," which accepts the fact that a person cannot know absolutely everything and that there are degrees of accuracy in a person's perception. "One casts his or her knowledge according to how he or she perceives it."

I saw that notion of perception as being alive in Hermann. His knowledge was shaped by his perception. His perception was moulded by his prison cell. He was examining and re-examining his life against a background of enclosure; reconciling his past freedom with his present imprisonment, while all the time his future whispered hauntingly, a great unknown, like a grey ghost in his ear. That may have been his biggest challenge.

So Hermann was a minister. It had changed his life. "I was not so religious before. As a child I had to go to the religious hours in Germany. As a Protestant you had to go through Confirmation. It's always in your life. You must go! Sometimes you don't have the right minister. Sometimes you don't have the right teacher. All my life I never was praying, just the last few years, since my last girlfriend left me."

With his new calling, he intended to help people. "It's not something I want to do, it's something I *have* to do. I see the problem[s] in here and … the problems between [an earlier girlfriend] and me. [In prison] I see men crying when the wife is home and alone. I see the men crying when a woman walk[s] away.… I see the men crying when they want to talk to their children and the children not allowed to because the woman doesn't want [them] to [see him]. And I say to them 'if you want your wife to stay with you and respect you, you have to show respect for her.'"

He had spent a lot of time speaking with the chaplain at Collins Bay, talking about helping other inmates, serving as a role model for them, guiding them to be better people, but he says he didn't receive the kind of support he expected. He was looking for the kind of shared commitment, an *esprit de corps* that would unite him with other religious leaders in the prison. But this didn't happen, and it caused him much disappointment.

16

Doing His Time

HERMANN WORKED IN THE INDUSTRIAL SHOP WHILE HE WAS INCARCERATED at Collins Bay. He was also involved in a new project that involved building computers. "This is a project to … teach people how to make computers. This could be a very important job for me," he told me during our last interview.

Hermann had at one point been a maintenance person in the carpentry shop, doing odd jobs. He was hoping to get back to that work when the current project finished a few months later.

I tried to call Hermann's case manager, to get his perspective on how Hermann was managing his life in prison. But there was no answer. When I tried to leave a message, I was told by the switchboard operator that they didn't take messages. This was a Friday. She asked me to try calling back on Monday.

"Will the case manager be in Monday?" I asked.

"I don't know. This is only the switchboard."

"Then how do I know that this person will be in?" I asked.

Dead air — the woman had hung up on me.

In my experience, this was the general course of events when you tried to contact someone at a penal institution. With few exceptions, most of the personnel were initially suspicious, then rude, aggressive, or, on occasion, just plain obnoxious. It seemed to me that they had a tendency to assume that anyone from the outside who was seeking information was unworthy of their time and effort, or that they were a troublemaker trying to find weaknesses in the institution. Or maybe it was just simply job-related stress.

§

While in prison, Hermann worked out, but the authorities advised him against teaching martial arts. He was told, "If you want to do something, you do it for yourself. But you don't teach it to anybody else."

There was a variety of sports and other activities offered at Collins Bay for the inmates to participate in. There was a disabled Olympics held at the facility, which attracted participants from across North America. There was a pool room, two weight rooms, and a large exercise yard. He told me there was also baseball, football (or rugby, he wasn't certain), and floor hockey. This was in addition to a library and the meetings of various religious groups ("I am the chairman" of one, he told me).

There were friendships there as well. He told me it was useful for lifers, especially those who have killed someone else, to develop friendships that would help them through their time. With respect to those who had committed murder, Hermann explained that "most of the time, it's an accident anyways, because most of the time somebody get[s] mad. It's very hard for somebody on the outside to understand why somebody get[s] killed."

He took time to compare his sentence to that of Karla Homolka: "This woman, she was helping her husband kill those girls and she got twelve years, and I, in my case, nobody was killed, nobody was hurt — and I get fifteen years! In this case, where is the justice in this country?"

I asked Hermann to clarify whether he received a fifteen-year sentence or thirteen years, as I had been told by his lawyer. He became annoyed. "I get fifteen. Okay? And she got twelve years for helping [her] husband kill those girls and maybe five or six others."

When I finally got through to Hermann's case manager at Collins Bay, he agreed to a phone interview, but on the basis of anonymity. He seemed like a decent guy, talkative, and his approach renewed my faith in the possibility that not all workers in the prison system were negative, suspicious, or abusive. He filled me in on the basics of life in an institution and explained that case managers are somewhat like account executives. They have a "client list" of between thirty to forty inmates, and they keep track of the programs in which they are enrolled. He would not comment directly on Hermann, citing the fact that all the information about Hermann was confidential.

The manager told me that when an inmate arrives in an institution, he is put through a battery of tests before being slotted into one of four categories:

1. Limit-setters: Those with a history of dysfunctional problems such as an inability to either find or hold down a job.
2. Situational type A: Inmates suffering from an alcohol or drug-abuse problem. These are conditions that are considered to be correctable with proper treatment.
3. Situational type B: Inmates whose crime is considered to be a once-in-a-lifetime event (although the case manager is restricted from stating it outright, there is a strong intimation that Hermann is in this category). Those convicted of crimes of passion, such as manslaughter, may also be in this group.
4. Psychopaths: Prisoners whose state of being lacks a conscience. These inmates are unable to fully realize the complete impact of their actions. They act out of immediate, self-gratifying motives that emphasize excitement and thrills.

Once categorized, a correctional plan for the inmate is outlined, taking into account the actions necessary for him or her to achieve certain goals: "The goal is a gradual release plan. They ... work toward lower security, then day parole, and finally full parole."

Inmates are also expected to attend school if they haven't attained grade ten.

The typical inmate is in his early twenties and has already spent several years in the system. Most are in a "real bad mood," the manager says with understated subtlety.

To get them into a mood where they can realize the impact of their crimes and move toward improving their chances at doing well once they're back on the street, they are offered a variety of core programs, which include living skills, substance abuse counselling, and literacy classes.

Probably the most important is the living skills initiative, which, in a broad sense, "helps inmates to expand their thinking process to include what someone else's reality is," explained the case manager. "They have a very narrow perception of what is going on around them. They can't relate to how their victims see things."

In one component, for instance, inmates are asked for their views on euthanasia. A vote among the participants is taken. Later, they are asked to consider two reasons why a person with an opposing viewpoint might feel the way they do. This is often the first time in their lives that inmates are asked to consider someone else's perceptions. It also helps to break many out of the "tunnel vision" that clouds their thinking.

Most importantly, it helps prepare them for the time when they face a parole board, when they will have to account fully for their actions. "There is a certain amount of tunnel vision [they focus only on themselves].... All they see is their reality. With their crime, there are certain aspects of it they cannot face. They can't deal with it. That's something the parole board is concerned about. The parole board members really put them on the spot. They ask that they account for their crimes, that they understand them, and that they realize how wrong their actions were."

The case manager explained that this can mean the difference between freedom and more months of incarceration. Would Hermann be ready when the time came? Was he moving toward reconciling himself to the pain that he had caused? The case manager paused. "That is something I can't answer. Confidentiality."

§

In my face-to-face interview with Hermann, the issue of friendships came up. "I have never [had] many friends on the outside, why [do] I have to make friends now?" was his answer. "I was always more or less a loner. I love to have my family, do my work. I love to go out for dinner, have fun, fine. But I have not any real friends. My attitude is here, and no one told me this, this is just how I feel, I'm on the right track. Just leave me alone. If you need my help, just ask me, I like to help. But I do my own time; I don't get involved in anything here, especially in the groups [who] like drugs. You end up in the hole so often, you get a bad reputation. I don't like it." His voice rose. "I don't need it! In this ten months, nine months I'm ... here now, you are the second person [to] visit me. My only [other] real visit, my sister come and visit with my sister from Germany."

He was hopeful that a pen pal, someone with whom he had been corresponding for a few months, would visit him soon; they were waiting for permission to be granted. There were (and continue to be) a number of pen pal programs run in conjunction with penitentiaries, offering inmates a chance to connect with the outside world. Hermann said he leaped at the chance to communicate with people outside Collins Bay, though he didn't offer any further details about his pen pal.

I was curious how Hermann felt as he looked back on the events of October 31, 1991.

"More and more I feel sorry, but I can't change it any more. My intention was really not to hurt anyone. In this kind of wild chase, people have got hurt, mentally. I want to apologize. I will do it personally. I feel sorry this has happened with the police, but my personal feelings is that a policeman, officer, whether woman or a man, make[s] the oath to become a police officer and um, come[s] into situation like this, chases or whatever, and someone goes so crazy like me, and was pushed ... shot at or whatever, or give[s] them a little chase, and then they say I pissed and shit in my pants [out of fright]. These people are not ready to become police officers. Better they quit the job and do something else."

I said nothing, waiting for him to continue. He took this as a negative and glared at me. "You are not seeing my point!" The truth was, I could see his point, from his perspective. I told him that I understood what he meant, but Hermann persisted. He pointed a thick index finger at me. "It's not that I'm angry, I'm not talking bad. It's just the feeling that if [as a police officer] you're not ready for your job [don't do it]. If you are wearing a uniform, you have to account for your actions. What I was doing, it could happen to anyone else."

The issue of the local police officers not taking advantage of Hermann's fitness studio still got under his skin. In his opinion, the police in Canada were weak, overfed, and lacked exercise, and he said, "John, this was my feeling at the time — to teach police to be strong people, mind- and body-wise. [You're] never going to be a good police officer if you sit for twenty-four hours a day, or twelve-hour duty ... sitting in a car driving around or sitting in a doughnut shop. You'll never become a good police officer. Then you come into a situation, any situation, and you become angry because you cannot handle these situations. There's so much in this country now, so much is wrong from my point of view. You know it. Everyone knows it."

Hermann waved his hands about in evangelistic fervour. "Everybody says your system stinks. But nobody knows how to do anything, nobody says anything, nobody knows how to change it. Now you know why I'm here. I wanna say something. I was stupid. To let [myself] down, [ruin] my good name ..." He realized he would have to wait to have an opportunity to make his peace with the police.

The fact that the police had the temerity to pull their guns on him was like a slap in the face to Hermann. He had come to his own conclusion that the police were inefficient, and as a strong, capable person, to be challenged by the police caused him great indignation. Despite the facts — the guns he had in his possession, his violent kidnapping of the limousine driver, his bravado in the banks, his aggressive, no-holds-barred shootouts during the chase — he derides the police for their cowboy mentality.

"I never realized that somebody had pulled a gun on me," he said, sucking in breath. "He [the police officer who gunned him down] pulled a gun on me! These people cannot solve the problem. This country is still like a hundred years ago where everybody [wore] a gun in cowboy time, the Wild West, wild, wild ... and the rules are with the gun. And this is the same way today. And the police, they are the same. In England, the police don't wear a gun and everybody have a good time." (Although, starting in 1994, London bobbies would begin wearing visible, hip-holstered side arms.)

I asked him if he felt any remorse. "I feel sorry in one way, and stupid in the next way. I'm here. I have to take my time. I have to help myself, because nobody will help me. I don't want to open my mouth!" He said the less he talked to others, the better. It was all about minding his own business.

Hermann told me his plans for the future included helping other people in prison "so they can cope with their problems. Not many people could understand that there are people behind the wall here who are good people too. You have to take a person by the hand and show them. I was the same way, too, before I came in here. I might stay in this area, because I see lots going on here [in Kingston]. I want to minister and I have really found what I'm looking for. [In my ministry] I'm allowed to have people. I am a real pastor like anybody else."

And what about the budgies?

"Yes," he said. He had been drawing pictures of budgies, and his sister had recently sent him a picture of his sheepdog. "The more I know women, the more I love my animals," he joked. His laughter echoed off the walls of the room.

I asked him about his children. He had three sons and a daughter. He told me that one of his sons didn't care about him, which hurt. He told me that his nine grandchildren, on the other hand, had been writing and telling him they loved him. He talked about his father and how his father avoided contact with him up until the day he died; Hermann didn't want that to happen to his relationship with his own children.

"When I get out [of] here and get a permit to visit … I will go back and visit my children, my grandchildren, [and] my family." As for the son who refused to contact him: "I feel sorry for him and I pray for him."

And what about Hermann's other children? He said that in general they had shown him some compassion. At Collins Bay, he spoke beseechingly of the need for them to respect him, even if he was behind bars. About one son, whom he wanted to provide with some kind of positive influence, he said, "I tell my son, you only have one father. You better smarten up … understand, think about it, you only have one life, one father." Hermann said he told his kids that, despite the fact that they had another father figure in their lives, a stepfather, "you really only have one father, who loves you."

That subject seemed to send him on an emotional tailspin, and his voice rose in anger. But after a few minutes he regained control and we talked about more mundane things, like the food in prison, which he said was acceptable but nothing special. As we left the room, the narrow corridor was empty. As we waited for the gate to open that would allow me out of this place, he talked to me about joking with the guards. He shoved the heel of his hand against my chest; it was a playful shove, but it was also a concentrated, focused little poke that I could feel.

"You see, this is how I joke around with the guards." His laugh rang hollowly in the open space by the guard room. One of the guards looked at him, gave him a wry, I-know-what-you're-up-to kind of smile, in what passed for prison collegiality. I watched Hermann walk away, the walk of an older man, with just the slightest limp from his bad hip, but his head was held high and his back was straight.

17

Wedding Bells

On Valentine's Day 1994, Hermann married Denise, a widow and mother of six from a village about twenty minutes north of Kingston. She moved to Kingston early in 1994 to live with one of her daughters.

A few weeks before the wedding, I spoke to Denise on the phone, and she expressed her concern to me about Hermann, with whom she began corresponding through an Ottawa-based letter-writing organization nine months earlier. Was she the mystery pen pal mentioned during our previous interview?

She was upset because Hermann had apparently been receiving death threats from other inmates. "Hermann got too friendly with some of the guards. Some of the inmates are after him," she told me. Hermann himself acknowledged that he was friendly with the guards in a jokey, back-slapping kind of way, which I had witnessed in my previous visit. But the other inmates didn't like it, Denise said: "A couple of them came over to him ... and told him not to turn his back."

She wanted things to run smoothly; she desperately hoped that their long months of first casual, later serious, courting, through letters and daily visits, would finally be fulfilled with the wedding. "I'm waiting for him to call me back."

There were plans to send Hermann to another penitentiary, possibly Joyceville, Denise informed me. This was confirmed by Collins Bay's Paul Donnelly, who told me after the wedding that Hermann was on a waiting list for either Joyceville or Warkworth, which were both nearby. "Right now he's in protected custody," Donnelly said. No details were given as to the reasons for the protection, but it certainly seemed to confirm Denise's claim of death threats. But for Denise, having Hermann close by and safe was good enough.

"We're a lot alike," she said. Denise's husband of twenty-three years had died two years earlier. She was close to Hermann in age (she was born in the mid-1940s) and, like Hermann, she had a large brood, including five grandchildren at the time, with "two more on the way."

It had taken her a while to get used to Hermann, she confessed. "At first I thought he was rather cold." But Denise, who was born in England and came to Canada as a child, reiterated that the pair shared similarities in attitude. "I could be saying one thing and at the same time he could be saying the same thing." She hinted at the fact that they were both focused on "traditional values." I asked her what she meant, and, perhaps wondering how her attitude would be taken, she waited until I offered "you mean the man playing a fairly dominant role in the household?" before agreeing.

"Yes, that's right," she said. "Some people don't like it. But it was the way I was raised. At the same time, I've also seen him cry."

Some members of her family were supportive of her union with Hermann, others were not. But Denise was stoic. When I asked her about the fact that Hermann wouldn't be out, free to walk around or to make plans and decisions about their life, until at least 1997, she replied, "I can deal with that. I found it very hard at first. But you make choices." Her immediate concern at the time was seeing that her man was safe. As well as just plain seeing him. "Before [the trouble with the other inmates began] it was five visits a week. In the past couple of weeks they've had two lockdowns…. It's getting to the point [where] if you're going through the metal detector and it beeps, they'll start into you." They were hassling her? Didn't they know her in there? Yes, she told me, but some [of the staff] were nicer than others. And when lockdowns occurred, the tension rose.

I asked her how Hermann handled the lockdowns. "He has his good days and his bad," she said. Lately it had been bad. During the latest lockdown, his television set had been confiscated as a "contraband" item. If there was a reason why, she was never told. Her understanding of the situation came down to a dozen words: "I think everybody in there is just trying to back-stab everybody else."

Photo by John Cooper

Hermann and his wife in Collins Bay Penitentiary. They met through an inmate letter-writing program, fell in love, and were married on Valentine's Day 1994. The marriage wouldn't last.

But when freedom finally came, they were going to have budgies (maybe) and definitely dogs. Hermann talked about dogs a lot. He really missed his Old English sheepdogs. And once Hermann's parole was finished, they planned to go to Germany for a visit — all part of an effort to break from the past. "We've talked about all this. I told him that once he's out of there, I want … things … behind us. It's something we'll never forget, but we have to put it behind us."

I asked Denise if she considered herself strong, courageous, and committed to a cause. "I don't think I am," she said. "I think in some ways I understand it [what Hermann did]. But he's got to learn to put that behind him and get on with it."

18

A Legal Perspective: Paul Stern

When I met lawyer Paul Stern at his office in the spring of 1994, he was exactly as I expected, professional to the core. His eyes were sharp, and there was just enough of a hint of well-heeled confidence to make one feel a bit intimidated. He had the poise of one of those professional people profiled in advertisements for scotch: The office: Bay Street, Toronto. The clientele: the famous or infamous. The scotch: Dewar's. At the same time, he could offer up little jokes and asides to make his clientele feel more comfortable, maybe squirm a little less as they faced their uncertain futures.

Stern watched as I sat, rumpled and uncomfortably bent over in a knees-to-chin pose of helplessness/supplication on the overstuffed, leather-clad sofa in his office. As I said, he was exactly what I expected a Bay Street lawyer to be; behind his office door, or somewhere out of sight, must have hung a tailored Harry Rosen suit jacket to go with his razor-creased conservative blue slacks. He wore suspenders over a crisp white shirt. His shoes were black patent leather with little tassels.

Permeating the office was the smell of fruit — oranges and grapefruit. A near-volleyball-sized grapefruit sat in a dish on a front credenza. "One of my clients runs a fruit stand in Florida," Stern informed me. He chuckled at this. Perhaps it was one of his stress-reducing jokes?

He was clearly not pleased with the outcome of Hermann's trial. And why would he be? Nobody likes to lose. But there's losing and then there's *losing.* Hermann lost, big time. If Stern wasn't bitter about it, at least it grated on him, despite his composure when talking about it. Equally grating was the fact that the Crown had appealed the sentence.

Stern called the result, a thirteen-year prison sentence, a tragedy. This was no glib excessiveness, the histrionics that one expects from lawyers. He said it with a sincerity that made it truly believable.

"I think it's a tragic thing … Hermann, no criminal record, so many years of hard work behind him, and with so much good behaviour behind him. I think it is tragic that at his age he finds himself in a maximum security prison where he is going to be for years to come, having lost essentially everything. All of his possessions you could put in a box. I think that is tragic. He is a charming man to me, a hard worker, a very proud guy who committed very serious offences, and that is tragic.

"I think it's a unique case, not just in relation to cases I've handled before. There are very, very few cases of older responsible people with no record committing a series of armed robberies. There are very few cases. It happens, but rarely.

"I think of some cases: there [was] a police officer in Calgary who went and did a number of armed robberies — six, ten, twelve, twenty, I don't recall — using his service revolver. Very unusual.

"And what Hermann did [was] very unusual. Then, with the chase that followed the last one, with the shooting in the general direction of the police, it's rare, highly unusual. You know you see people shooting at the police, people you could almost predict if you look at their criminal record, that eventually they are going to be shooting at police. Hermann does not fit in that category at all. He was a great supporter of the police in many ways, had great respect for the police; he had friends that were police officers, that's what makes it all unusual from many perspectives, but from a purely criminal lawyer point of view, it's unheard of in this type of case. One hundred and twelve different charges!" As he said this he stabbed at the air for emphasis, one precise index finger crooked just so, poking at the air. Had a jury suddenly appeared out of thin air and listened to him speak, I had no doubt they would have been convinced. The emphasis on his delivery increased, in pulse and tone. It was a rapid-fire staccato before he took a breather to pause and look at me as if to say "Does that make it clear to you?"

Paul Stern, Hermann's lawyer: a tough and incisive Bay Street legal mind. Faced with banker's boxes full of evidence, he tried to get Hermann the best deal he could.

He continued. "I mean, look, this case was a tremendous amount of work just in terms of trying to understand what the allegations were and what the evidence in support of those allegations was. To be able to discuss it in a meaningful way with Hermann meant that I had to understand it."

He listed the components of the case, his voice serving to bullet-point his remarks: The tapes of the radio transmissions and transcripts; an infrared videotape of the chase, shot from the police helicopter; a re-enactment video covering the chase, with views from both helicopter and police vehicles.

Stern's biggest questions arose from the issues of shots being fired by Hermann and hitting police vehicles; while vehicles may have been hit, the all-important attempt-murder charges were difficult to prove, from his perspective. As well, officers' testimony varied greatly, he says. "Fifteen to twenty officers giving evidence about what happened ... each had a different recollection, which is human nature ... people recall things differently."

As well, there was Hermann's testimony that he was in the United States when several of the robberies were committed, evidence of which was examined during the preliminary hearings and negated.

Stern said he spent a lot of time on the case, even hiring a law student (who later became a lawyer and worked in London, Ontario) whose background as a private investigator was a "great help." The student logged more than forty hours of work, adding to the hundreds that Stern would log. The law student "ran around trying to get the videos in hand." The videos became essential for viewing and interpretation, because of the discrepancies between police recollections and Hermann's own. Stern said the evidence helped to clarify exactly who did what, and it helped him build his defence, because the case hinged on the question of Hermann taking a gun out, firing it at police, and then moving on. Was he drawing on the police first? Was he intending to kill them? Stern knew that analysis of the video evidence would prove useful.

He tried hard to get a digitally enhanced image of the infrared pursuit video that was shot from the helicopter, but was unsuccessful. He had hoped it might lighten the weight of evidence against his client.

"Well, my hope was to get someone with a digital enhancer, but we could not get anyone to do it. They do it with the space shuttle. We just never got to that point, and I don't know if it is possible — and perhaps it is not. Remember in the United Kingdom recently, with the video with the boys with the little boy? [He was referring to video used at the 1993 trial in the death of James Bulger, a Liverpool toddler who was lured to his death by two ten-year-olds.] But they never digitally enhanced that either."

He paced the room and ran a hand over his head. He looked out the window at Bay Street far below. His voice took on a staccato beat. He didn't stop for breath.

"I had this fellow [the law student] off trying to find out.... we ended up with this lab which did a lot of work on [the video], slowing it down, filtering, breaking it down into segments. All kinds of stuff, but it still left doubts from my point of view. It didn't prove what I felt it had to prove ... to offset the police evidence, which was unanimous on certain things. To offset it we had Hermann and we had the video. Hermann, I had to bear in mind, had been shot and his recollection might have been poor. So, that took a lot of time, that whole phase, it was a case that went on and on and on, back and forth to jail and phone calls and more paper and more paper, police officers' notebooks. Because, you see, in a case like this there is a great temptation from a lawyer's point of view to just give up and get steamrolled because there is abundant evidence in the chase. I mean, there is not a lot to work with. Hermann was there, the chase happened, and shots were fired."

It came down to producing a series of computer-generated images of the scenes in which Hermann was firing at police. "We ended up in the final discussions of the case using the computer generated things I had to guide the discussions. I don't mean me and Hermann; I mean me and the Crown, the judge. And faxes were going through [from] here to them as we tried to focus in on a solution to the case. The judge made himself available and was extremely helpful in keeping the discussions moving."

Pleading guilty meant a withdrawal of some of the other charges. And the upshot was not too surprising. "It was a sentence. He pleaded guilty, so that the finding was guilty. Registering a conviction was not something I could complain about under the circumstances. The sentence itself I thought was stiff. I personally felt, knowing Hermann, that it was heavier than it had to be ... for a man in his fifties."

Technically, it was considered a sentence of fifteen years. It was adjusted down to thirteen years to reflect the fact that Hermann had spent fifteen months in pre-trial custody. Stern emphasizes that the "time served while waiting" for trial was not deducted from Hermann's sentence, as is the case with some sentences. And pre-trial time, because it is served in detention centres — more jail-like, transitory in nature and more challenging than penitentiaries — is often considered as double time. So, while on the record Hermann's sentence was thirteen years, in reality it was more like fifteen and a half years, Stern told me. "So, the judge imposed a sentence designed to be in his view the equivalent of a fifteen-year sentence. From many points of view this is the equivalent of a fifteen-and-a-half year sentence. That is a heavy sentence for a first offender — even though the crimes are serious — it's a heavy sentence for a man his age."

He rose. He seemed spent, and his eyes looked tired.

"It's a heavy sentence for a man of Hermann's age who has nothing, whose life is in a couple of boxes. It is a sentence that leaves him with … I mean he has hope and one of the charming things about Hermann is that he has some get up and go and some willingness to try again and get up and do better again, but he does not have as much time as someone who's twenty. So the judge considered all of the factors, I think. We will see what the Court of Appeal says. Considering all the factors raised by the Crown and by the defence, that is what he [the judge] thought was fair. I can't be critical of him … my own feeling is that it could have been less, but the prosecutor's feeling is that it could have been more."

19

The Trial

When it came to Hermann's trial, while a lot of preparation went into it, when it finally arrived, it lacked the drama that one might expect. Hermann pleaded guilty to everything. The court held preliminary hearings to examine evidence and listen to the testimony of witnesses, and then there was a ten-month wait before sentencing. There were few surprises, except for the sentence — a total of thirteen years (in addition to the fifteen months already served in Toronto-area detention centres). The sentence was deemed too short by the prosecution and too long by the defence.

At the preliminary inquiry at Ontario Court (Provincial Division) in April 1992, Hermann's ex-fiancée, Lana, took the stand. Nothing out of the ordinary came out of this Examination-in-Chief by Crown Attorney Mary Ellen Cullen. Lana confirmed her on-again-off-again common-law relationship with Hermann and her knowledge of his businesses. But she strongly denied any knowledge of the robberies.

Cullen's questioning was tight and direct. If Lana had prior knowledge of the robberies, Cullen's aim was to get her to open up about them on the stand.

Lana told the court she had been told by Hermann in 1991 that he was doing security work at the Honda plant in Alliston and also in the United States. But she never knew the name of his American employer.

During the questioning, which delved into matters of joint residency, defence lawyer Paul Stern asked the court: "What is the relevancy of probing this witness's background and where she's lived? I object on that basis given the charges. It's not a matrimonial court."

Judge T. Wolder allowed the questioning to continue in order to establish Lana's relationship with the accused at that stage.

Lana confirmed that while she helped out at the fitness centre as a receptionist in the evenings, she knew nothing else of Hermann's financial status, only learning of his March 1991 bankruptcy later that year.

"Do I understand also, in the summer of 1991, the two of you purchased a weight-loss clinic franchise?" Cullen asked.

"Yes, we did."

It had been a $10,000 investment.

"Where did the money come from?" Cullen asked her.

"It came from Hermann ... he just told me it was money from his security work in the United States."

The pair also took a vacation at Hermann's expense, the cost of which was unknown to Lana, who also stated that she didn't know what his income was from the fitness centre. She told the court that they were planning to be married, also at Hermann's expense. Lana maintained she didn't ask how he got the money to pay for things.

After his arrest, there was a total of $3,000 in Hermann's account at the Bank of Montreal in Alliston. Another account in the Alliston Toronto Dominion Bank contained $35.

Lana was at the fitness centre when Hermann was arrested. There was a buzz around town that he had been arrested, so she had phoned several police departments and then the hospital in Brampton in an attempt to find out what had happened. She had last seen Hermann the previous Monday; she said he told her he was going to the United States and so she picked up his car at the Sheraton Hotel near the airport.

"Did it surprise you that it was there ... are you curious at all about why it was there?" asked Cullen.

"I was curious ... but I did not ask him."

During Cullen's questioning of Lana about her phone calls to various police departments, Paul Stern stepped in with a poignant set of questions designed to present the Hermann/Lana relationship of intended marriage as one on a par with that of a married couple, and worthy of the same treatment under law, such that spouses cannot be compelled to testify against each other:

> Your Honour, before the witness is asked by the Crown about discussions had with the accused, I mean, clearly we're on a discovery mission by the Crown at this stage in the case where the woman is being asked about conversations she has had with a person with whom she co-habited in what's colloquially called a common-law relationship, but in the circumstances where there was a wedding planned … where there was an intention of marriage, which [there] was — of course, there was an arrest, which frustrated those plans, depending on how you look at things, but it did. Now my friend [Cullen] plans to ask a lot of questions going into an area that in my submission approaches an area which is in law privileged, being the remarks made to a recipient spouse. Now I know there's case law dealing with this in a context where a marriage is dissolved. Here we have a rather different context where the marriage is planned, was going to take place.

The judge asked Stern for any case law "to persuade me that the privilege which is extended between married spouses also extends to common-law partners even where a marriage is contemplated?"

Stern replied, "No, but as a matter of policy the same case law that supported the formation of the privilege between married spouses should in my submission extend to this type of situation. It's very different from the case law that says when a marriage has broken down then the policy underpinning that privilege no longer applies. That the more modern cases that we've had in the past years, that's what they say, for good reason. There's no policy basis to uphold the privilege when the marriage has broken down. Here we have the reverse situation, where there's every policy basis to uphold the privilege because the marriage was intended and very approximate so the policy that underlines that law is here, whereas in those other cases it's not."

Judge Wolder was not convinced: "[T]he policy basis is that the courts in the past have had to balance the communications within the sanctity of the marriage as opposed to the requirement to obtain real evidence, and that principle, even in recent cases, one that I had ruled on last year and one that now the Supreme Court of Canada has dealt with recently, goes the issue of where, even between spouses, where a spouse wishes to testify, has not been compelled, that a spouse is still competent and that spouse also has rights under the Charter. I am not aware of any case law, and if counsel cannot provide me with any case law to persuade me that policy that they referred to, the historical policy, should also apply to common-law parties.... I ruled there is no privilege in this case and I am going to allow the Crown to continue."

Lana reaffirmed that Hermann did not talk to her about the robberies.

"I'm going to ask you quite a direct question, ma'am," said Cullen. "As you can appreciate, there are a number of robberies that have gone on with lots of money outstanding.... You talked to Mr. Beier. Do you know where that money is?"

"No, I do not," she answered.

Not much more could be said than that. Lana exited the courtroom, and at the same time, she left Hermann's life. The thought of her still pains Hermann. "She took so much from me," he said, although he clammed up tightly when I asked him to elaborate.

My later attempts to speak with her at home and at work were met with shouted, angry words: "You call me again and I'll get my lawyer after you!"

At Hermann's sentencing on February 4, 1993, presided over by Justice Kenneth Langdon, the facts were read out directly, mechanically. There were no histrionics, no impassioned pleas for leniency.

The facts are a matter of public record: On April 25, 1991, at 10:30 a.m., Hermann robbed the DUCA Credit Union in Orangeville. It was good choice of a place to rob — he had performed construction and finishing work on the inside of the credit union when it was opened the year previous and so was familiar with its layout.

"At the time, he was disguised wearing a black shoulder-length wig, a bandanna around his forehead, dark-rimmed glasses, and a black scarf, which covered his nose, mouth, chin, and neck area," Crown Counsel Mary Ellen Cullen told the court.

Armed with a handgun, and carrying a garbage bag, he ordered the staff to the front of the credit union and told them to open the registers and fill the bag.

At gunpoint, he ordered staff to the back of the credit union, and told them to open a small vault.

Unfortunately, he gave employees a tip-off when he ordered a staffer into the washroom, which was unmarked; it could only have been known to an employee or someone else who knew the layout of the building. He had been there to do some additional work because work originally done at the credit union was not up to par.

Other than waving his gun around, Hermann was not aggressive, despite the threat of the firearm. "During the entire time the accused was in the credit union, the employees described him as being very calm and soft-spoken, and at all times he had the gun pointed toward them." With the money from the tills and the vault in hand, he left. His total take from that particular location had been $13,143.

Hermann left the credit union and got into a stolen Honda, which he had taken from the Honda plant in Alliston, where, just a month before, he had terminated his part-time employment as a security guard. As a result of his work there (Hermann even had a letter of reference from his supervisor), he knew the route the security guards took when they checked the premises. At 5:15 on the morning of April 25, a guard on a routine check had stopped his car to check on a building because, as he told the court, he noticed that "something seemed to be amiss with one of the locks." Hermann took that opportunity to jump into the car and drive away.

At 12:50 p.m. that same day, Hermann pulled up in front of a branch of the Canadian Imperial Bank of Commerce in Nobleton, a village in York Region, north of Kleinburg. After entering the bank carrying a green garbage bag and pointing a black handgun at the tellers, he asked for money and also whether the safe was open. He was still wearing the same disguise he had on during the previous robbery, and was described as "very calm during the course of this robbery," Crown Counsel told the court. His total take at the Nobleton CIBC was $2,797.

Fifteen minutes later, Hermann drove up to the CIBC branch in Schomberg, just north of Nobleton. This time he was a little more direct, banging the butt of his gun on the counter to get the attention of the staff, and then passing over a green garbage bag.

"Witnesses described the accused as being collected and also aggressive in manner," the court was told. The garbage bag was passed down the line of five tellers, each taking their turn adding money to it.

William James Brydon testified at the preliminary inquiry in Newmarket on May 1, 1992, that he was at the CIBC branch that day; as a self-employed businessman, he was there to pay his Goods and Services Tax. He described the gunman as being dressed in black, with a black toque, a scarf covering most of his face, and wearing a wig and what looked like makeup on his face. He said that the gunman was calm and rational, uttering only a few words, like "fill it up" as he banged the gun on the counter.

"It's a small town, and I thought it was a joke at first, but he walked a little a farther down the counter and hit it again, and I realized there was something wrong then."

A teller was crying, and Brydon stated that the whole incident only took "two or three minutes." He said the gunman called out "nobody move" in a strong German accent as he left the bank.

It being a smaller town, Brydon had left his keys in his car, and he recalled being concerned that the man would steal it. But he testified that he watched as the suspect got into a car that was parked behind his own, backed it up, eased out into traffic, and headed along the road that led out of town.

The total take at that location was $5,462. The stolen Honda he drove that day was recovered in Barrie later in the spring.

The court was also told that on July 31, 1991, at 9:55 in the morning, a gunman arrived at the Royal Bank in Beeton, Ontario, just south of Hermann's home town of Alliston. He was driving an airport limousine, which he had commandeered, at gunpoint, an hour and a half earlier. Ten minutes before his arrival, a Loomis Armoured Car Service delivery of money was made to the bank. His arrival was timed perfectly with the arrival of the cash, as the bank's time-lock was kept on a bank-standard five- to ten-minute time delay.

Dressed in black and wearing a black wig similar to those used in subsequent robberies, the gunman covered his face with a white dust mask, entered the bank, and pointed a semi-automatic gun at teller Monica McConnan, demanding money. "This isn't a joke," witnesses heard him say. "I want the money." Then he tipped back the gun slightly, making it look like he was getting ready to fire. He was provided with $2,400 in cash.

It wasn't enough.

"The carrier was just here and I want the parcel," he said of the Loomis drop-off. The parcel was passed over and the gunman exited the bank and got away with a total of $96,400 in cash.

It's been said that it's hard to defend the indefensible. And that's true in Hermann's case. A few months later, he started to ring up purchases — purchases made with cold hard cash. The court read out a list of cash purchases he made during August and September of 1991 — and these were made in spite of Hermann having declared personal bankruptcy in March of that year. On August 8, he purchased a car for $5,370.20. On August 14, he purchased a franchise for a Beverly Hills Weight Loss Management Centre for $10,000. (A good investment, it seems. According to a survey done by U.S.-based Marketdata Enterprises and publicized in *USA Today*, commercial weight-loss programs were worth $1.7 billion in 1994, just one small portion of a massive weight-loss industry valued at $33 billion in the U.S alone. It turned out to be a smart move by Hermann, as it was one enterprise that ended up doing rather well.)

A call I made to the weight loss centre's head office in Waterloo was met with some interest. "Of course we know that name [Hermann's] here," Gloria Goersch, the company's public relations representative, said with a chuckle. But her initial friendliness soon waned. I was transferred to company controller Robert Miniou, who said that any requests for information would have to be cleared by the Board of Directors.

"What if all I want to know is some basic information?" I asked. "The length of time the company has been in business, for instance?" I also expressed interest in finding out if the franchise was still in operation.

I told Miniou that all I had been able to find out about the company was from an article that had appeared in the *Globe and Mail* in the summer of 1991 about a lawsuit that had been launched against the Nutri-System weight loss people. The court action had focused on misrepresentation of the Beverly Hills name in an advertisement that was supposed to be referring to the Beverly Hills Diet, not the weight loss clinic (the ad listed "unsuccessful" weight-loss programs). Mr. Miniou couldn't — or wouldn't — say whether the company had won that case.

And with regard to my request for company information, he said, "Sorry, but everything has to go through the Board of Directors."

I then asked him if he knew anything about Hermann. "This company was taken over by new management not too long ago," he told me. After a brief pause, he continued. "And we don't know anything about anything that happened prior to that. We certainly don't have any information about this person you're talking about."

Between August 6 and 9, 1991, Hermann also mailed money to his four children in Germany — $1,400 worth of deutschemarks. On August 16, he booked a trip for two to California for $1,382. The trip was taken just a few weeks later, September 5. On August 21, he paid $1,800 in rent (first and last month's for the weight-loss clinic). Between September 16 and 18, he had his car painted and a new roof installed for $1,380. On September 20, he deposited $1,000 into a bank account at the National Trust in Alliston — the deposit was made in brand new (and sequentially-numbered) two-dollar bills. Also in September, he booked fourteen tickets for a return flight from Frankfurt to Toronto for seven adults, seven children, and one infant, for the Christmas holidays that year, a grand total of $10,647. The payment for those flights was due on October 31 — the day he was arrested.

On October 30, Hermann kidnapped limousine driver Nasib Singh Mander, then dumped him out of the car in a rural area. Court was told by Mander that Hermann had threatened him with death.

And, as detailed earlier, the next day Hermann went into action for the last time. Wearing a wig and fake moustache, and dressed all in black, he robbed branches of the Royal Bank in Georgetown, Rockwood, and Guelph. The subsequent chase was long, difficult, and dangerous; it was punctuated by shootouts, by Hermann advancing on police officers with machine-like intensity, and it finally ended with Hermann being shot beside a farmer's field. While the money taken on October 31 was recovered, none of the money from the October 30 robberies was ever found.

There wasn't a lot in this official account that lawyer Paul Stern could argue with. The facts as they were read into the record were fairly iron-clad. But he did raise some questions.

"The number of shots that were fired by the client and by various police officers remains a matter of ... I think it is fair of me to say ... there is some uncertainty. Different people have different recollections. Some officers I know who clearly fired six shots, for example, honestly believe they only fired two. That is the state of affairs. With respect to my client and his own recollection ..." Stern's point was that, in the heat of battle, memory deteriorates, sometimes to the point where it can affect the credibility of the evidence provided to the court.

"Much of what you have heard ... is on the video, so Your Honour will be able to see some of these events and draw your own conclusion from what you see, particularly dealing with the situation with Officer Stennett ..." Stern told the court. "This is the Halton police constable whose vehicle went into the ditch. The video shows that, and when you look at it, I would ask Your Honour to bear in mind that my client does not believe that he fired at that officer after his car went into the ditch." Hermann admitted to firing twice, and Stern proposed that it was possible that Stennett might believe that there were more shots fired at his car as it went past Hermann into the ditch. Stern was raising doubts as to the veracity of anyone's memory, given the circumstances that day.

Later, Crown Counsel Mary Ellen Cullen would remark that the court had sworn statements from police offices at the scene, statements entered into the record at the preliminary inquiry, that they saw the accused "shooting at the Stennett vehicle when it was in the ditch."

And of the final dramatic scene between Constable Erskine and Hermann Beier, Stern stated, "Mr. Beier does not believe he fired right at the end of the chase, but he was hit [when the vehicles collided], he was virtually unconscious, and certainly I know that Officer Erskine has testified that Mr. Beier did fire at him. The video shows what happened at the end to some considerable extent. It is unquestioned Mr. Beier fired at those officers at some point, but I alert you to that."

Regardless of any doubt that may have been introduced into the proceedings, in the final analysis, the nitty-gritty details were moot — Hermann was found guilty, and he was given a sentence that the court felt was in line with the seriousness of his crimes.

20

Granola and Sandals: Beard, Carlisle

Hermann had two civil lawyers handle the matters that were not covered by the services of a criminal lawyer, such as the distribution of his possessions.

As mentioned earlier, Beard, Carlisle was a wife and husband team of lawyers in their thirties who ran their practice out of an office in mid-town Toronto — an area that straddled Bloor Street north of the University of Toronto campus and was home to a mix of hip young urbanites and university students. They had moved recently from an office on Parliament Street, across from Regent Park, a neighbourhood encompassing Canada's oldest and largest social housing project.

On the way into their new office, I passed through a low wrought-iron gate, up a short flight of stone steps, and through a heavy wooden door topped with a half-moon of stained glass. Inside, a poster of a pop-art painting of Queen Elizabeth decorated a wall painted shiny white. A secretary with ruby lips and disdainful eyes directed me, with a wave of her blood-red manicured nails, up a flight of burnished stairs that creaked with each step.

Paula Beard looked the part of an earnest lawyer. She wore her hair in a practical clip; round glasses perched on a face unmarked by makeup. James Carlisle, a former biologist turned lawyer, with his fuzzy beard, didn't seem to have a hard edge anywhere.

According to Beard, the pair became involved with Hermann because the convicted bank robber was trying to have a pin in his hip repositioned following surgery he had undergone while he was being held at the Maplehurst Correctional Facility and Detention Centre in Milton, Ontario.

"He was injured rather severely and he was seen by a doctor," said Beard. "In fact, one of the things that we were doing for him was trying to [fix] a technical problem more than anything else.… When he was … at Maplehurst, he wanted his doctor to take the pin out or to reposition the pin, [but] his doctor was not willing to do that because Maplehurst is quite a distance from Mississauga [where the doctor had his office]."

Beard was trying to get the provincial Ministry of Corrections to either send the doctor to Maplehurst or send Hermann to the doctor's office in Mississauga. The ministry was unwilling to do either because of the fact that Maplehurst was a detention facility. According to the officials there, because of cutbacks at the Ministry of Corrections, there were things that a detention centre could not do because it was a short-term facility, and one of those things was sending inmates out for medical treatment.

"The frustrating thing from Hermann's point of view is that Maplehurst happens to be both; it is Maplehurst Correctional Facility and Detention Centre. He just happened to be on the wrong side of the building [in the detention centre]. If he had been a hundred feet away on the other side of a wall [the correctional facility], the ministry would have paid to send him back to his doctor to have this done," said Beard. "Instead, they refused because he was in a detention centre, not a correctional institution. I believe he was told by the nurse there to just wait until he got to Millhaven, and I believe that is how it has been resolved."

Beard rifled through a file folder until she got to the appropriate page. "The other thing that we are doing for Hermann is attempting to clarify for him his position with respect to some property. He has a long-term relationship with a woman and [her] daughter, and although he is not technically married to her, it is [considered] a common-law relationship, and for various reasons there seems to be some difficulties there. He is attempting to get her to release some of his goods to his sister — there is a car he wants his nephew to drive and some personal goods. She, the common-law wife, is represented by a lawyer, and one of the things we've been doing is writing to that lawyer and attempting to get his goods out of the hands of the common-law spouse and into the hands of his sister, where he wants them to go."

Hermann first contacted Beard and Carlisle in December of 1992.

"I can't recall exactly how he was referred to us, but there was some issue at the beginning whether or not we would assist Mr. Stern with the case because James does most of the criminal work and I do most of the civil and family work. So, originally when we were talking to Hermann, it was [about] whether he needed our assistance with his criminal problems, and subsequently he decided that, no, he would not. Then he had us doing other things. There was at one point [talk] about a potential civil suit against the police."

This was the $2-million lawsuit against the police that Hermann had mentioned in a letter to me. Beard said that any litigation against the police for damages had to take place within six months of the incident. "Unfortunately, because he was in hospital for a [long] … time, and because he received inadequate legal advice for a period of time once he was released from the hospital, by the time he was able to discuss this with someone and retain somebody who was in a position to do something for him, his six months had already run out. And the problem with limitation periods is that they are absolute."

While other legal time frames are more flexible, the Supreme Court of Ontario had stuck to the six-month rule, noted Beard. "There was at that point very little we could do. Apart from that, there was a real concern that he had not had a trial, he had not yet been sentenced, and there was a real concern that if he brought an action against the police it would not indicate any sort of remorse on his part and a judge would probably take it amiss. I feel that this is completely unfair. I mean, putting aside anything else, if you are assaulted by a police officer you should have the right to recover … whether or not there were other circumstances involved."

With the odds stacked against them, often the advice that clients are given is to drop their case against the police, said Beard, adding that showing remorse is the only way to go when you are up on major charges such as the kind Hermann faced.

"In a criminal proceeding like that, the judge would say, 'You can't be very sorry for what you did, Hermann, if you're suing [the police]. You must think you were partially in the right, or you would not be bringing this civil action.' It would be very difficult for a judge to divorce his mind from the two quite different aspects of the case. I think you can be very sorry for being involved in criminal activities and be very regretful and realize your mistake, and still have a legitimate grievance against somebody who came after you with a gun and injured you severely."

21

In the "Bay" with Mr. and Mrs. Beier

Hermann came to Canada for clean air and open spaces. He enjoyed swinging a hammer in the sunshine and tooling along country roads for mile after mile in his big car. But when time for fresh air and exercise arrived in those days after his incarceration, it was spent in a three metre by three metre cubicle in the Collins Bay compound, surrounded by brick. The walls were more than three metres high — too high to see over. I could easily imagine a lone prisoner playing handball against the wall, like a scene from a movie.

Sure, an inmate could see the sky. He could crane his neck and strain his gaze upward, and thrust his face toward the thin, washed-out blue. He could hope on a grey day that a stray shaft of sunlight would land like a butterfly kiss on his eyelids, nose, and lips, and bathe him in warmth for a few minutes. He might have been able to watch a few cottony wisps of cloud scud by, starting at one line of bricks, disappearing at another. He could time them, five, seven, maybe ten seconds across, from stage left to stage right. And in the summer he could hope that an errant breeze would find its way down the shaft, cooling him for a few precious seconds before its vortex weakened and died.

At that time, Hermann was allowed outside for only a half-hour a day. Another thirty minutes was allotted for showering and personal care, but the remaining twenty-three hours each day were spent in lockup.

On my next visit to Disneyland, I met with a case worker (who didn't want to be identified) in a small, nondescript office. "He's a bug," she told me, referring to Hermann. "He'll work you with the same questions every day." That was her opening statement. But for all the questions I asked, the answers she provided were generally vague, clouded by brick-wall impenetrability.

She lit a cigarette, and I asked her what type of questions Hermann kept asking. She sighed, and the sigh drove out a plume of smoke. There wasn't much forthcoming. I asked what her opinion of Hermann was, and she told me that what struck her the most was his attitude about himself: "He has a very grandiose manner. He feels that he is very important, if not in anybody else's mind, then in his own."

But was that so surprising, in a place where everything was skewed toward reflection, where the day to day routine was a mirror that surrounded the prisoners, where every day Hermann was forced, no matter where he turned, to see images of himself, who he was, who he wanted to be, how others wanted him to be?

"Hermann has a problem with women, you see," said the case worker. He had apparently had problems with his previous case worker due to his habit of "speaking down to her," she told me as she drew on her cigarette, letting the smoke curl lazily out of her mouth. But this case worker was different. "I demand that people speak to me cordially," she said, shifting position and putting her feet up on a file drawer that had been pulled out.

At that time, in early 1994, Hermann was already eligible for ETA, or escorted temporary absence. For example, should a relative die, he would be allowed to attend the funeral, as long as he was in the custody of two security officers. However, absence from the facility was restricted to eight hours or less.

(In 1995, he became eligible for UTA, or unescorted temporary absence, giving him, at the discretion of the parole board, up to 48 hours of freedom. In 1996, he would be scheduled to come up before the parole board. A psychological profile and risk assessment would be presented at that time. Hermann would have to show remorse for his crimes. He would have to have an exemplary record of behaviour while behind bars. If he met the criteria, he would be allowed to spend up to six months at a halfway house, leading to full parole — if all conditions were met and he maintained his law-abiding behaviour — in 1997. Full parole would require regular checks with a parole officer, whom he would have to report to once a month.)

But it was his attitude that put him at jeopardy, said the case worker. "If he ever expects to get parole, he has to get one trait — he has to learn to be humble."

But humble Hermann wasn't. She told me that he saw himself as being "very grandiose." As she said this, an unsettling, satisfied smile appeared on her face.

I asked her how she felt about his recent wedding. "I've done hundreds of weddings," she told me, which I took to mean that she had witnessed many weddings inside the prison. "I'm just not comfortable with them."

She wouldn't elaborate.

I asked whether it was because some of the women who married men behind bars were much like their husbands. Were they looking for love in all the wrong places, as the song goes? Were they tied into a pattern of behaviour that made them idolize criminals, turned on by the machismo of men who hated "the system," tough guys who didn't give a damn about anything, least of all the law?

The case worker only giggled. "I'm not permitted to counsel her," she said, referring to Hermann's wife. She added that she would have liked to have said a few words to her, though, maybe given her a bit of the low-down on Hermann.

§

When I arrived to speak with Hermann and his new bride that day at Collins Bay, they were already waiting for me in the reception lounge. As with other inmates and their visitors, they had managed to create that particular cocoon of privacy in a public place. I stood by the door of the narrow observation booth as two workers filled out forms, talked on the telephone, and watched monitors flanked by rows of white lights. They had an air of bored concentration about them. It was a familiar look. I saw it in office workers all the time — the eyes focused but oddly lapsed, a flimsy curtain behind which true thoughts scurry about busily, the lines of the mouth taut, the forehead smooth.

I waited patiently. There were lots of calls on my behalf: Calls to the head case worker. Calls here. Calls there. I was used to the delays by then. While I waited, I watched the happy couple, Mr. and Mrs. Hermann Beier, through the mirrored glass. They were seated at a table, their chairs drawn a little away from it so that they faced each other. Hermann had his legs open in a V-shape that took in and contained his wife. It was an act of possession, of restraint, Hermann holding his love close. He cradled her hands gently in his. Then he leaned over and began kissing her passionately. I was stunned. Because he was well over fifty, I figured Hermann had been in the saddle too many days for that kind of stuff. I figured that he would be content with a cuddle and a peck on the cheek. Boy, was I wrong!

I had to admit he had gusto, and he was going for it with every gram of energy — and every bit of strained propriety that could be pushed against the ever-present vigilance of the guards. His wife, with the blue-rinse saintliness of a small-town grandmother, closed her eyes and arched her head back slightly in meeting-room rapture.

When Hermann came over to the window a few minutes later to get change for the coffee machine, he saw me. "Are you going to watch us through the window, or are you going to come in?" he said cheerfully.

"I'm still waiting," I told him.

When I was finally allowed in, Hermann embraced me with a bear hug and then patted my tummy. "You lose weight!" he said. I was greeted with a smile and a small hug from his wife. We exchanged pleasantries, and then went on to talk about more serious matters.

Hermann complained that he sat around "twenty-four hours a day. You can't go anywhere." He was allowed five visits per week, but during four of them he was separated from his wife by a barrier. Only one was a personal-contact visit in the common room, which is what they were enjoying that day.

Hermann told me that when the two finally met face to face, after corresponding for a couple of months through the prison's pen pal program, they had hit it off immediately. Whether or not she was the pen pal he spoke of previously, I never found out.

We talked about the wedding. It was fast, said Denise with a laugh. The ceremony had taken place in a house trailer. Because it took place during lockup, the wedding party consisted only of Denise's son (as best man), her maid-of-honour, and a justice of the peace. After ten minutes, everything was done and the marriage certificate was signed. Coffee was then served, and within the hour everyone had left except Hermann and his bride.

"I was shaking like an idiot," said Hermann, admitting to a case of nerves on his wedding night. "I was shaking like someone running in a marathon."

Hermann maintained that the marriage would help him in an emotional way. He told me that the prison psychologist said his moods were sometimes up, sometimes down, and felt that his marriage would help to stabilize these swings.

Denise was hopeful for the future. "At first I found it very difficult. But now, I think it's going to make us stronger. I have no conflict."

At that point, Hermann jumped in: "From my point of view, for me, I'm getting used to this [being in jail]. A person who has married someone in jail must have a very strong will, very strong love, and a strong mind to do this. Because the moment that this man is in jail for four years, they must have so much love for this person to cope with this problem. It's not easy for somebody to do this."

Denise was unemployed, but was looking for work as a bookkeeper. Her daily routine consisted of looking for a job, looking for an apartment, and visiting Hermann. She had five grandchildren at the time, with two more on the way.

"Do you want a coffee?" Hermann asked me, plunking some change down on the table. "I like to have coffee when she comes … [but] you don't get … good coffee here [in the regular units]. It's no good here either [in the lounge], but it's coffee anyway."

As Hermann was getting the coffee, he chatted with the man in the booth. Denise pushed back her hair and adjusted herself in her seat. She looked very delicate, thin and a bit fragile.

When Hermann returned, he told me, "We have a lot of plans. We can't talk too much in the future. You have to live in jail … there is one law, you live day by day, tomorrow can be finished for a man, he could be killed or whatever. But we'll have a house or whatever to live [in]. [Because of] all the years that we missed together, we want to enjoy them." His plan was simple: work and enjoy life. "I don't want to teach [apprenticeships] anymore. I will go where I can," he explained. "Go into cottage country, where people need somebody to fix the cottages or appliances. Little things, you know."

When I brought up the subject of birds, he said, "When you breed birds for thirty-five years, you miss them. I miss them very much, but here I cannot have them. I talk to [Denise] about it already, and she said, 'I don't care as long as we are together.' She loves animals. She would like to have a dog. Me, I would like to have my sheepdogs again."

But Hermann also told me that he wanted to travel when he got out. "When you have a dog, you can travel, but with birds you have to stay around."

And he didn't know if the folks at the Budgerigar Club would take him back. "I heard from [Kathleen], and she said 'Hermann, come back, we need a new president in the club again, the club broke down [after his arrest]. When you were president, the club was flying high.'"

He told me he was disappointed because he had lost his address books. Apparently, the guards had moved his belongings when he transferred from Millhaven, and he claimed that "somebody [had] tossed it out the window."

But he told me that some people still kept in contact with him. "At least five or six people are thinking of me and still writing to me."

He had recently run into some problems with his television set, as well, and had traded it away to another inmate in exchange for a television set that turned out to be stolen. That "new" set was subsequently taken away from him. He called it a "stupid thing that happened," and blamed himself for a lapse in judgement. Then he skipped back to the day of his robberies and raised the question of whether his moods had been affected by ingesting too many calcium-based antacids. I told him about the research that disproved the claim of hypercalcemia.

"But it was too much," he insisted. "I was taking the Chinese power pills at the same time. I lost so much of my strength, and then [I ate] more to get back my strength. My body was so screwed up that something happened [to my mind]."

He told me his favourite movies were always those starring Charles Bronson and Bruce Lee — especially Bruce Lee. He preferred martial arts or bare-knuckle fighting to guns. "For me, violence is when somebody goes with a gun." He made a *rat-a-tat-tat* sound and pointed his index fingers like pistols. He explained to me that the martial arts are not violent: "Bruce Lee practises martial arts. That's true martial arts."

I then brought up the subject of Hermann's ex-fiancée, a woman he had been going out with and was ready to marry around the time of the robberies. She had issued a legal order to keep him away. "I think, and I'm guessing, that she wanted to have a man with a lot of money," Hermann said. "And [when] she met me, I had three businesses. [Then] she found out … [that] I didn't have this kind of money. From one minute to the [next] minute," he said, as he snapped his fingers, "she dropped me like a hot potato.

"I was a person who [gave] a damn about myself. So I was floating, not normally my normal way, I was floating low, low-floating. So many things happen. These people [his ex-girlfriends] hurt me so much. I don't want to point the finger so much, but these people … when somebody wants to hurt you so much, you don't turn around and put a knife in their back."

He turned to Denise. "She built me up with her laugh, to the old Hermann [that] I was before. I never would realize today, pinch me if I'm dreaming, that I would meet somebody real. For years I was looking for Mrs. Right. Now, after awhile, I see that they were really after the money or whatever. Now I have nothing … and she [Denise] started loving me, and she … married me. We help each other, emotionally. That is what we need."

He believed at the time that Joyceville, where he had been told he would be moving shortly, would be "a much easier place."

22

"EXCITEMENT AND EASY MONEY"

YOU CAN FIND DOZENS OF ACCOUNTS OF BANK ROBBERIES IN ANY NUMber of newspapers in Canada and the U.S. each month. In 1993, there were more than three hundred reported in the Greater Toronto Area alone, though by 2006 that number had dropped to 202 and the following year to 122.

Some bank robbers are just a little more stylish, more brazen, or more foolish than others.

Movies like *Bonnie and Clyde* and *Dog Day Afternoon* lift their subjects, however immoral or dirty, to mythical heights — bank robbers almost always engender some measure of sympathy in the Hollywood treatment. There is always something in them with which viewers can identify.

Although most "true crime" books deal with mass murderers and psychopaths, bank robbers still hold a measure of intrigue — it's one crime that many people can visualize themselves doing.

In Canada, some stories and their subjects have gained a measure of prominence. For example, Dwight Pichette may be Canada's most famous habitual criminal. In his autobiography *The Diary of a Bank Robber*, he details his life following his release from prison in 1981. His freedom didn't last long, but his incarceration proved a boon to his creative spirit.

Pichette had served several years for a variety of offences, including armed robbery and kidnapping. In the book, he writes about his attempts to curb his alcohol and drug abuse through membership in

Alcoholics Anonymous. Pichette also tried to improve his situation by taking college courses and working at two jobs to keep himself busy, but despite having a wife, a child, and a dog, and what would seem to be a stable life, his old addictions and lifestyle eventually caught up with him and he descended into a vicious round of alcohol and drug abuse. In the midst of an alcoholic blackout, he conducted his first post-prison bank robbery early one morning. He got away, and continued a cycle of drug abuse and robberies.

The spree ended when he was arrested and charged with a myriad of offences, including possession of an explosive device, kidnapping, and extortion. He was sent back to jail. By May 2001, he was in prison on fifty-eight counts of robbery and robbery-related charges, for which he was serving fourteen concurrent life terms in Victoria, B.C. And yet he was a prolific writer, and in addition to *The Diary of a Bank Robber*, he had published two more books. A fourth book received an arts award before its publication. But during a supervised leave, he escaped, and made two more bank robbery attempts. These crimes earned him an additional two life terms.

If there were ever a typical lifetime criminal, Pichette was it: a person caught in a cycle of crime, driven to it by drug abuse, a need for excitement and easy money.

In the book *The Stopwatch Gang* (MacMillan Canada, 1992), journalist Greg Weston chronicles the saga of a trio of Canadian bank robbers — Paddy Mitchell, Steve Reid, and Lionel Wright. Far from being habitual criminals, they lived comfortable middle-class lives. Still, they did have one thing in common with their criminal-minded brethren — a need for quick cash. And you might throw in a desire for excitement, too.

Mitchell was a suburban family man whose failed attempt to run an aluminum siding business drove him to find an easy way out to bankroll his lavish lifestyle. Reid was an ex-hippie searching for a cheap high and the money to keep it going. Wright was a nerdy, introverted office boy who disliked drugs and alcohol; preferring instead to watch television and read history books; he became Mitchell's avid sidekick.

With Mitchell as the mastermind, the trio conducted an Ottawa gold theft and several bank robberies across North America, and also concocted a cocaine importing scheme. Their escapades culminated in the theft of hundreds of thousands of dollars from a San Diego bank in 1980. During the robberies, they were characterized by witnesses as polite, charming, and clever. Two of the men were arrested, charged, and later convicted for their crimes; the third, Paddy Mitchell, was on the lam for years until his 1995 arrest in Texas.

In 1981, journalist Heather Robertson produced a profile of Ken Leishman, a pilot with a penchant for bank heists, in *The Flying Bandit* (James Lorimer & Company). Leishman, who disappeared in 1979, flew from Winnipeg, where he lived a moderately successful life as a middle-class sales agent, to Toronto to rob banks. He also carried out the theft of $400,000 in gold bullion at the Winnipeg airport. In the book, Robertson compares Leishman variously to the Scarlet Pimpernel and Robin Hood. He became, for a short period, quite a celebrity.

In 1980, PaperJacks Ltd. published *Heist: Famous Canadian Robberies* by journalist Fred McClement. In it, the author imbued his stories with flair, style, and catchy titles, from "The Wild Ones" and "Barefoot in the Snow" to "Vaults of Vancouver and the Chinook Bandit" and "The Fat Man Cometh and Honest Rewards." In a section titled "Largest Heist in Canadian History," the author writes of a $6-million theft of money orders from a branch of the Canadian Post Office in Ottawa.

23

Joyceville Penitentiary, March 13, 1995

THE AREA NORTH OF KINGSTON, ONTARIO, IS INDEED FARMING COUNTRY. From the highway, all I could see across the rolling landscape were several barns. If not for the big Correctional Services Canada sign on Highway 15, from a distance I could have easily mistaken Joyceville Penitentiary, and its neighbour, the Pittsburgh Institution, for one large factory farming operation. But the facility's true purpose became very apparent as I got closer and was able to make out the razor wire, guard tower, and several strategically-placed surveillance cameras.

The main building was about three storeys high, painted white and bordered by green open spaces and trailers — I was later told these were reserved for conjugal and family visits. They were placed within the confines of three-metre-high double chain-link fencing topped with the ubiquitous razor wire.

I parked the car, and then proceeded to a small square building. Once inside, I approached the smoked glass that separated prison officials from the public. The glass had a little window cut into it, which contained a metal speaker box. Immediately I sensed that I was being watched, but I was unable to see my observers. It was a very unsettling feeling. Where was I supposed to go? Who was I supposed to talk to? Muffled voices filtered out between the slats of the speaker box. Before entering, I had to wait for a buzzer to sound. To get anywhere, I had to stand in front of a door, any door, and wait for a buzzer to sound. I felt like the family pet waiting patiently for someone to let me in. And it required patience and quickness to grab those door handles and get the damn things open before the buzzer stopped.

Once inside, I spoke to a heavy-set man behind the counter. The thick moustache creeping over his thin upper lip made him look to me like a cross between Captain Kangaroo and comedian Martin Mull. "You want to see who? Beier? You're not down on the list," he said, arching his salt-and-pepper eyebrows and scratching his nose with a thick forefinger.

I was thinking, *Give me a break. I made the appointment, then double-checked it, then confirmed it again two days ago.* But I kept quiet. As was true at the other penitentiaries where Hermann had stayed, I had the overriding feeling that it would not be in my best interest to hassle the officials.

I explained that the person in charge of visits, Rae Gately, had confirmed via telephone that I was cleared for a visit that day. He called Gately and received the appropriate clearance, then signed me in. After that, he became more civil, even friendly. He instructed me to go into an adjacent glassed-in room, where about ten other visitors were already waiting. "Put your cash and your jacket and any valuables you have in a locker," he instructed, adding that I could keep up to fifteen dollars (loose change, no folding money) in my pocket for use at the vending machines in the room.

I stood at the waiting room door, again anticipating the sound of the buzzer. Once inside, I stashed my gear in one of the lockers and took a seat. The chairs were wine-coloured and badly worn. The corners of the armrests were frayed and there were odd stains here and there.

The other visitors did no more than glance at me as I entered. There was an Italian family — an older woman dressed in black, and four others who I presumed were her children, two daughters and two sons. She looked tired as she leaned lightly against one son, speaking in little breaths of Italian. The other son sat apart from the others. As if recently injured, he used a cane. He was having difficulty with it.

Elsewhere, a young woman in her twenties combed her hair in front of a mirror mounted on one wall. She was wearing a short grey skirt, cut way up, and high heels. She pushed her wispy blond hair back and studied her face in the mirror. She was wearing a lot of makeup.

Joyceville Penitentiary. By the time Hermann entered the facility, he was in the final stages of his incarceration. But the pressure and regimentation of day-to-day life was getting to him.

A small girl, about four or five years old, with equally blond hair, danced a little jig about the room, as if to create her own fun, in that distinctive, unselfconscious way of small children — I figured she was likely the woman's daughter. Another woman in blue jeans and a loose-fitting white shirt was blowing bubbles with her gum and exchanging sexual innuendo with another woman.

"It's Bubblicious," she said. "Jesus, this stuff is starting to hurt my jaws." Her chuckling laugh carried just the hint of a twang.

"Your jaws better work okay for your old man," the other woman said. "Haw, haw." Perhaps there was a conjugal visit in store. The two of them, as well as the woman at the mirror, broke out in laughter.

I waited about twenty minutes until it was my turn to go to the interview room, which was located in the main building. The man at the counter waved a metal-detecting wand around me after I had emptied my pockets. He went over every inch of my body carefully before giving me the go-ahead.

"Where to?" I asked.

"Out the door, down the path, then to that big building over there."
He nodded out the window to the main building. "Up the steps and
straight through."

The room I entered reminded me of my old high-school cafeteria —
the ceiling was about four metres high; the bottom of the wall was bricked
up about two metres, and the rest of the way to the ceiling was pale stucco.

I surveyed a raised area that overlooked a lower level that was fur-
nished with teak tables and brown chairs, many of which were worn
down to the underpad.

In the interview room, two women behind a glass partition kept
watch over the proceedings. Their job was to deal with the inflow of
visitors and maintain a restrained vigilance over the room; they were
watchful, but friendly.

Vending machines stood at each end of the raised area. To the side
were shelves filled with a few worn toys: a Mattel See 'n Say, a pile of
blocks, and some teddy bears and dolls.

Next to the shelves, on a raised platform, was a small black-and-
white television. A muffled jumble of words streamed from a talk show
— Ricki or Maury or Montel was squeezing some juicy dirt out of somebody. But the television was just background noise, because the real business here was visiting people you hadn't seen in a long, long time, and
nobody was watching it.

Everyone in the room seemed to avoid any eye contact. They looked
at the floor, or the ceiling, or the steel door at the side of the room through
which the inmates entered.

The women behind the counter were cheerful. One smiled at me and
said, "Just sign in. Lots of signing in around here." She looked away, then
back again, casually glancing at my name. "Have you ever been here before?
No? Who are you here to see?" When I told her, she just said, "Oh, him."

A doorway at one end of the room led outside to an area surrounded
by a five-foot-high chain-link fence. Three rows of picnic tables sat on
the scrubby grass. I noticed that the woman in the short skirt and her
friend from the waiting room were already outside smoking.

I took a seat inside. I listened to, but did not register, the humming
cicada-drone of the television set. I heard but ignored the sounds of
hushed conversations. I waited for the heavy door to open.

A few minutes later, it swung open and a young man entered. Not Hermann. The man was welcomed by the Italian family I had noticed earlier — most likely another son. He appeared to be in his early thirties, and wore a grim expression. He looked as if he was determined not to break down in front of his family. He tapped a black patent leather shoe (strangely out of place with his blue jeans and red shirt) nervously on the green tiled floor. He waited a moment, looking at his family, then bent down to hug his mother. This was followed by kisses — right cheek, left cheek, right cheek again. His mother started to cry, putting her head down, her chin tucked in tight against her black overcoat. She choked off her sobs, perhaps not wanting her grief to be a public spectacle. The sisters kissed their brother and begin to cry too. Each brother then took his turn. The mother turned away from her inmate son and buried her head in another son's shoulder; her head bobbing up and down. This time there was no sound as she wept.

Finally, the inmate son lost control. Like a scene in a movie, he reached over and clasped his mother's hands in his. Tears flowed in two trickling rivulets from his eyes. A stray tear fell on his shoe as he kissed his mother's hands.

I turned my gaze away, back to the heavy steel door. Another inmate entered, bringing supplies for the vending machines. He was big and muscular, with thick biceps exposed by sleeves that had been rolled back to the shoulders. Like a splash of runny ink, a weeping blue tattoo, its image smudged by time, decorated his upper arm. He wore his hair in dreadlocks; the longer braids at the back held together by a small elastic hair band the colour of a ripe cherry. He brought boxes stacked high on a push cart to the vending machines. His face was passive; there was not a twitch of emotion. He looked at no one in the room. His non-committal look was finally broken as he smiled and nodded to another inmate, also on a job duty mission, who passed by and offered a quiet hello.

Another man entered through the steel door and looked around. There was a grey-haired woman wearing a neck brace sitting in the raised portion of the room, and when he spotted her, his pace picked up, as if he were trying to appear jaunty, unworried. He was tall, as equally grey as the woman, with rheumy eyes and sharp lines that carved up his face into a living, breathing jigsaw puzzle. The two embraced, and he sat down heavily in a chair. I tried to imagine what this guy was in for, what he had done. He looked like somebody's grandfather. What could *my* grandfather, *anybody*'s grandfather, possibly do to break the law?

The door opened again and this time it was Hermann. He looked much older. Since the last time I'd seen him, his beard, which had had a few grey streaks in it, had become fully grizzled. I wondered if it was stress, or just a sign of his age.

His hair was still quite long, but instead of the jaunty pirate-style ponytail, I noticed it had been cut in a choppy and ragged style. He no longer looked like the aging, hearty rogue of years earlier — an "old hippie," his clients used to call him, smiling when they said it.

He could have been mistaken for a gentle department-store Santa Claus on his break, if not for those eyes. They seemed haunted, and haunting. He looked around the room, past me. I had to come closer before he recognized me; it had been a year since our last face-to-face meeting.

"Oh ... John. Where is my wife? Where is [Denise]?" he gasped. I told him I hadn't seen her.

"I thought maybe she would come," he said.

Self-consciously, he stuffed a thick hand into the pocket of his blue jeans and pulled out a stub that showed that he had a visitor scheduled for that day.

"But it doesn't say who is coming to visit me," he said, scratching his head. "That's the problem." He was clearly disappointed.

We moved outside, taking a seat at the far edge of the yard, at one of the picnic tables. When we sat down, I noticed that dozens of names were scratched into the wood: L.S. ♥ P.B., R.T. ♥ W.M.

It was a mild day, winter lengthening into spring. There was laughter in the yard, couples embracing. The children — the little blond girl and two others, a boy around her age and a younger girl — were playing in a makeshift sandbox.

A mixture of melting snow, cigarette butts, candy wrappers, and bits of chewing gum formed a wet paste on the grass. I glanced up at the double chain-link and razor wire that surrounded the sitting area. It was a lonely, surreal place, a place that was at once depressing and outlandish, like a strange and disturbing dream.

A couple to our left were engaged in the heaviest petting they could get away with in this public forum. Everyone else in the area appeared not to notice, diplomatically giving the couple a comfortable sphere, a free zone in which they could be themselves with each other.

This was one of the remarkable things I noticed about the inmates and their families — they seemed to learn very quickly to ignore the things that were going on around them. This feigned ignorance provided a neat little bubble of privacy that offered an ersatz sanctuary to folks who seldom saw, touched, or conversed with each other.

Hermann shifted stiffly in his seat. I could tell things were not going well. He had been focusing his energy on getting out — away from his unit, away from the institution. He was looking either for a transfer to another location, perhaps next door to the minimum security Pittsburgh Institution or to another work farm-style facility such as Beaver Creek, or to get out of the place altogether on the temporary absence program.

Since his arrest, Hermann had been incarcerated for three and a half years at that point, taking into account his initial time in hospital, his stays at the detention centres in Toronto and Milton, and time served at Millhaven, Collins Bay, and Joyceville. He was now identified by a number: 064286D.

The longer he stayed, the more the prison reminded him of a military base, he said. "You get told ... when to get up, when to eat. Everything." That rankled him. "I can't accept this. I'm not this kind ... I'm not this kind of criminal. I did something wrong and I end up in here. Now I'm in here and living with all kinds of people — wife and child abusers, drug dealers."

He saw so many things happening there, he said — drug deals, guards that manipulated inmates. When he tried to bring up the subject of guard misbehaviour at Collins Bay, it had led to death threats and a transfer to Joyceville. "Here I see the same shit. Guards buy drugs and all other kinds of shit in here. If you don't bring something in [for the guards], things can happen. Guards want to have sex with the inmates' wife or girlfriend." He spoke of guards fancying an inmate's woman, telling that inmate to have her meet them at a local motel; otherwise they would file a scathing report on the inmate's "misbehaviour." And he told me that "one guard at Millhaven, he made recommendations [for example, on inmate requests for temporary absence] for money. He made a lot of money. You pay him and he does things for you. For them [the guards], bending the law is the main part of their life."

At that time, Hermann was waiting for his opportunity at 48-hour temporary absence (TA). To date, he had been denied. He was considered to be a risk, and because of his upcoming appeal, nothing was happening. He had to wait until the appeal was over and the decision was made before he could be granted or denied a temporary absence. He saw an inconsistency in the approach of the officials — his unit manager and case worker — to his situation. He claimed that some of them said he was "too quiet," that he didn't mix well enough with others; others said he was "too talkative" — essentially a "shit-disturber."

He told me that, throughout all of this, his wife had stood by him, and he was confident she would, no matter what the outcome.

He also said he had a few friends on the inside, though he hesitated to call them close friends. They were "friends in a certain way," he said as he turned his face toward the weak sun, closing his eyes for a moment. "But the system says you're not allowed to have contact with other inmates. I know a few people from the chapel."

Hermann lived in Unit 2, Range 3A. The door of his cell was opened at 7:00 a.m. each day. His morning began with breakfast, which the inmates prepared themselves in a common room. From 8:00 until 11:15 a.m. he worked, issuing supplies, such as cleaning materials, to the other inmates, and making deliveries within the institution. Then he would have a break for lunch, followed by a head-count of inmates at noon, then a cleanup of the common room. He resumed his duties at 12:30, working until 3:45 p.m. At 5:00, there was a second head-count. Dinner was then served, cafeteria-style. The evening was spent in whatever activities interested the inmates — Hermann usually went to the gym, when his aching body could manage it, or sometimes into the yard outside. At 9:30, the inmates were instructed to clean up the yard. Cells were locked at 10:45 p.m. Day after day after day, the pattern was the same. The only breaks in the routine were the family trailer visits, medical appointments, or visits from friends from outside the institution.

Hermann's cell contained a television, a radio, and a typewriter. His other materials, including his wood-burning set, had been confiscated at

Collins Bay, then "lost," although he suspected that somebody had stolen them. As he told me this, he fingered the laminated wooden cross that hung from a leather thong around his neck.

He told me his closest friends there were a "Native person and a Chinese person. They 'muscle' me to go down to the gym." He patted his tummy and told me he needed the exercise, needed to get back in shape. His hip was bothering him, limiting the amount of exercise he could do before the pain would set in. At one point, when he got up to go over to the fence to speak briefly with another inmate, I noticed that he walked with peg-legged stiffness. Operations to repair his hip, knee, and a hernia had been scheduled for sometime soon, he believed. Hermann would be turning fifty-four that August.

He returned to the table and eased himself down onto the bench. On the other side of the fence, several sparrows chirped merrily. One tough little bird, its beak full of dried grass, flitted by, landing momentarily on the fence top, balancing like a child's toy; it tilted its head toward Hermann, then flew away. Hermann looked at it, briefly, and I thought of his love for his budgies. I thought he might smile, but he didn't.

Hermann told me he was waiting for approval of his application to move into Unit 5. He explained that that unit was less regimented — inmates had their own keys to the cells and there was an "open-door" policy. Waiting could be a frustrating process, though, and he was finding it difficult to get the necessary approvals. He felt that several of the officials were against him.

"Certain people, like the guards, don't want to help you. A guard said yesterday 'We are paid to keep you and we want to keep you as long as possible.' These people can make your life miserable."

At another table, two inmates and their partners reclined on the table top, puffing away on Export As and Colts, one of the men gently touching here, there, copping swift little feels of breast and buttock, a small bit of behavioural brinksmanship in the yard. A woman's voice suddenly crackled over a loudspeaker, asking them to stay off the table tops. The voice was smooth and firm, and the word *please* was emphasized. "What's the fucking problem?" one of the inmates said, but not loud enough for the correctional staff to hear him. It was a rare show of bravado in a place where the inmates generally kept their eyes to the floor or in the "dead space" immediately in front of them, intent on doing their duties and their time. No doubt his retort was intended to show his woman that, while he followed orders, easing his body down onto the picnic bench, he didn't have to like it.

The little blond girl was singing "*la-la-la-la-la*" in a thin, piping voice as she wandered around the yard. Her mother, the woman in the tight skirt, had removed her jacket to reveal a tank top, pale, sloping shoulders, and a tattoo on her right arm; she leaned into her man, digging her tongue deep inside his mouth.

Her partner, tall, square-shouldered, his blond hair pulled back into a ponytail, leaned equally firmly into her. His hand gently massaged her arm over the tattoo. Occasionally the heel of his hand eased inward and grazed her breast; like the inmate on the picnic table, he did what he could to get closer without breaking the rules. The woman reached up and caressed his goatee, which sprouted in ragged glory from his chin. The little girl continued her singsong chant, oblivious to the activity.

Hermann did not look. It was clearly an unwritten rule: you left other inmates and their visitors to themselves.

The woman who had been chewing the bubblegum in the waiting room was embraced by her man. He stood behind her, manipulating her spine, massaging her shoulders. She smiled, revealing a couple of missing teeth.

Hermann spoke to me about his children. He has tried to maintain contact with them. "My son Michael finally wrote a letter to me after two years," he told me sadly. "I feel a little bit badly. Maybe it's just the situation. It's tough to call to Germany." The last time he telephoned his children it had cost him almost eighty dollars, he said.

The thought of this made him angry. Money was the root of his problem. The acquisition of it was supposed to have taken him away from his troubles. Then his focus shifted to lawyer Paul Stern. With a rueful look, he told me that the lawyer had urged him to shut up; otherwise he'd never get out. There was probably some truth to that.

Hermann turned to the topic of the motivation behind his crimes. "I never do something in my life without a reason," he told me.

"To make a statement?" I asked.

He hesitated, as if the words that he was saying (and he had said those words to me before) were going to create more problems for him.

There was wariness to his manner. He slammed his fist into his palm. "Yes!" he finally said. "Yes!"

The act of driving a car was an active metaphor in Hermann's life. Driving meant freedom: open roads, blue skies, no worries, and, most of all, nobody looking over his shoulder and telling him what to do. It meant power and control: from zero to sixty in eight seconds. Driving meant money: getting from one place to another for his renovation work. It meant women: the Eldorado was a powerful, macho sex symbol, fully loaded. And, eventually, driving spelled the end for Hermann as well: a well-tooled Lincoln against more than a dozen police cars; a sleek black bird trying to evade a flock of hungry, wailing gulls.

He told me, "When I come to Toronto in 1984, I drive down the road, make a wrong turn." He tried to get into a parking lot to turn around. He told me that, while waiting to make the turn, a woman ran into his car with hers. She was crying, he said. When the police arrived, he said they were nice to him, but he claimed that he was "tricked" by the police, who issued him a ticket and forced him to plead guilty.

He tapped my arm. "You see my point?" He told me his relationship with the police deteriorated from there, because of the frequent stops during his back-road sojourns in the Eldorado and other "intrusions."

I looked up. The little blond girl had stopped her singing, though Mommy and (one presumes) Daddy were still fondling each other on the picnic table. The little girl had been joined by two more children — an Aboriginal boy of about six wearing black jeans, rubber boots, and a red checkered shirt, and a smaller, dark-haired girl with big eyes the colour of chestnuts. They played together in the makeshift sandbox. They clawed, pulled, and pushed the sand about with toy rakes and shovels. The sand was still damp from an earlier rain, but they persevered, building it into piles. They talked to one another in squeaks and chirps.

"I'm an easygoing person," continued Hermann. He reverted to the bravado he demonstrated two years before, shortly after his sentencing. "Don't step on my tail, or I can be a wild animal. Don't tell me I want to kill somebody. If I wanted to kill somebody, they'd be laying out on the road. I was chased like a wild animal and then I turn around and I bite back. It's pissing me off, when they come to me and accuse me of these things."

Photo by John Cooper

In Joyceville Penitentiary, Hermann was looking with anticipation to the end of his incarceration. While there, he suffered from stomach problems stemming from being shot by police, and had turned to eating simple, natural foods whenever possible.

He was getting cranked up, the engine revving, the Eldorado's pistons pumping and ready to cut loose. In his mind, he was heading for the open road.

"How does a man who works overtime, day and night, to build a business, and then he gets accused of bank robberies just because of this and that?"

I looked at him blankly and he laughed heartily. "I'm telling you way too much!" He slapped me on the leg, a hard smack, but delivered in a good-natured, avuncular way.

"This is frustration," he added, his mood becoming clouded again. "They provoke you to do things, screaming and violence or whatever, just to keep you here." He kicked at the dirty grass, littered with cigarette butts. The sky had become overcast and the air had taken on a distinct chill.

"Guards take food from here, they take steak and chicken, and they take clothes and cleaning supplies." Each of his words was etched by acidic hatred of the guards.

His feelings toward his father resurfaced at that point. He never had an opportunity to reach that cold, distant man. "You know, he was a prison guard, too. He never said 'You are good, I'm proud of you.' And he never, ever [said] 'I love you.' And still I want to show my father I do something, something good."

He paused, looked away. He stared through the two sets of chain-link fence, toward the parking lot. There were several cars parked there, a collection of oversize Hot Wheels toys in a toy-box of colours — blues and greens and reds and greys. His mood suddenly changed. "You really realize what you miss in life. I'm getting over this," he said in reference to his relationship with his father.

"You must have had a better relationship with your sons," I said. He agreed. He had tried hard, he said, to do the right things in life. When he was a teenager and his girlfriend got pregnant, he married her. His oldest son was born in May of 1958.

All his life he had tried to do the right thing, and in his mind and his words he was turning back toward himself, reflecting on his responsibility — shifting from guards to father to sons to himself. "Now, all this, I don't want to say that it's their fault."

"Whose fault? The authorities?"

"Yes," he answered. "All whatever I do is my fault, my own actions." For a moment, there was a sense of absolute clarity in his words.

As we made our way back inside through the waiting room, I noticed that *The Beverly Hillbillies* was playing on the television. The room echoed with canned laughter. The toys sat untouched. I looked at one inmate as he played with a baby about six months old. "That's nice," I said to Hermann, gesturing to the man with the baby. "It's nice for people to be able to see their families, their children, here."

He looked at me pointedly. "Prison is no place for little kiddies. They should not be here. It is wrong."

§

Two months after my visit, I received a letter from Hermann. Gone were the neat, simple drawings of crucifixes, birds on the wing, rolling hills, and sunsets that once decorated the top of the envelopes.

Instead, the envelope was plain, and in the return address corner he had typed:

HARLEQUIN MINISTRY
P.O. Box 880 Suite 3-A-15
Joyceville, Ontario
K0H 1Y0 Canada

I figured Hermann must be using this as an "official address" when he was writing letters, such as the one he wrote to the government of Germany to petition for a disability pension.

The envelope contained some photocopied documents. One was a letter from the German government, denying him a German pension — Hermann was ineligible because his Canadian citizenship nullified any legal connection to his motherland.

The second was a copy of a complaint form. Several times over the past few months, some of Hermann's mail had been opened by correctional officers. So he had dashed off an inmate complaint form, demanding discipline for the offenders. Instead, a neat handwritten note on a response form offered an apology and an explanation that some correctional officers, new to the unit, lacked familiarity with the proper procedures.

There was also a letter. It was the standard length of Hermann's letters: two single-spaced lined pages in sometimes grammatically challenging but understandable English. In it, he provided details of his life, the day-to-day issues that came up, such as the situation with the Toronto lawyer whom he had written to, asking him to take his case against Corrections Canada and the police. The lawyer had refused. Hermann was dismayed. "What is going on in this country?" he wrote. "Is no one for right and justice? [Are they taking] mostly easy cases?"

Also, he claimed that the officers in charge of his unit continued to give him a hard time. "Here the incharged [*sic*] officers for me C.M.O. + C.O. II are playing heavy games with me. Would be too long to write all things down.... Still no answer [to] my request to move to Unit 5."

He also told me his relationship with his wife was strained, mainly because he worried about her health. A shared intent to make the marriage work was their strongest link, he said. They planned to move away from Ontario when he got paroled.

"[Denise] and I decide to go — move to the West Coast. Here in Ontario I wouldn't get any peace [from] the police. Our goal will be to live in peace and harmony so long [as] we can."

Helping Hermann move toward that sense of peace and harmony was Pastor Gary Reynolds, a Protestant chaplain at Joyceville. Reynolds met regularly with Hermann and saw him at church services.

"He comes down and I see him at least once a week privately in my office for a talk," he told me over the phone. "He comes to the services regularly."

Reverend Reynolds was a member of the Pentecostal Assemblies and ministered in the prison system as a Protestant chaplain. He was one of the few people in the institution whom Hermann genuinely respected. Hermann said Reverend Reynolds had helped him to better understand himself and his motivations.

Even after almost four years, the prison environment continued to be a surprise for Hermann, said the minister. "He copes with it the best he can. It's certainly true that he's not used to the hostile environment that a prison represents. It's not only a hostile environment, but a bureaucratic process where inmates become not a person but a number. But he deals with it definitely very well. He's very much *not* a part of the normal criminal element that you see in a prison."

That part of prison life — the illicit drugs, drinking of homemade hooch, violence, and surreptitious deal-making — was very frustrating to Hermann, Reverend Reynolds said.

He also admitted that the guards may not take as much interest in an inmate's well-being as, perhaps, a chaplain. "There is a tendency [for guards] to simply work with inmates and not see them for the people that they are. The individualism and the personal side of any relationship [between guards and inmates is] basically shot."

The strictly controlled atmosphere of prison underscored the depersonalization process. "It's so much a loss of your own freedom, the loss of your own mobility. And destiny, too, I suppose. You have really very little control over that."

Hermann was dealing with two issues at that time: First, the prison system and its effect on him. And second, he had to come to terms with his crimes, learn to feel remorse for them and recognize — and deal with — the root cause of those crimes.

"We deal with the immediate issues that are at hand at the moment," said Reverend Reynolds. "I more or less up until now have helped him deal with issues relating to the institution and with his marriage. [And now] he wants to go over some of the things he's done."

But unlike other professionals in the field, Reverend Reynolds said he preferred steering inmates away from the overriding sense of being a victim, though it was clearly acknowledged that they did become victims when placed into an artificial system of control like a prison, away from the natural forces that shaped human behaviour in outside society.

"I would say remorse is the lost commodity when it comes to inmates. Most are dealing with the issues day to day. We have a system that is so program-oriented. All of these programs tend to shift blame from the inmate to the addictions or circumstances under which they were raised. And the inmates feed into this. They say 'I'm a victim because of my background or because of my addiction or whatever.' That may be true," Reverend Reynolds adds, "but they must also feel remorse for what they have done and be willing to pay retribution, in one way or another, to the victims of their crimes."

To help move inmates through this process, the minister was running a prison program called Healing for Damaged Emotions. It dealt with self-concept, family origins, and depression. Hermann was a regular participant. And Reverend Reynolds saw some positive things coming from it. Whereas in the past his concerns were only immediate in nature, Hermann now spoke of his background.

"He has talked to me about his childhood," he said. "And he has spoken of his strained relationship with his father."

The minister viewed this as a positive first step toward bringing Hermann full-cycle to understand his actions and their consequences.

24

The Operation and the Appeal

On June 16, 1995, Hermann underwent surgery to deal with a problem with his hip and to fix his knee and buttocks. "My behind looked very butchered," he told me in a letter. It was the first operation performed on him since the emergency procedures done shortly after he was shot by police.

He related further details about the experience to me in a letter: "Also I have three holes in my left knee, where they put a scope in to see what is wrong with my knee." He found out later that he would eventually have to undergo knee replacement surgery.

According to a study by Dr. Kenneth Kizer of the University of California, and reported in the *Globe and Mail* on June 24, 1995, the average cost to treat a patient in the United States for a non-fatal gunshot wound is US$52,000. Using that as a standard, it would mean that Hermann's wounds have already racked up hundreds of thousands of dollars in medical costs.

Hermann's hip was operated on after the robbery. In a letter addressed to Hermann, his surgeon, Dr. John Rudan, outlined the results of additional surgery to remove a bone-connecting screw that had come loose and was causing him pain:

> You had a non-union of your greater trochanter [the top of the femur, in the area where the large leg bone fits into

the pelvis] as a result of the gunshot injury. The surgery was performed in order to gain healing of the greater trochanteric fracture. This was carried out. As a result of your surgery, your trochanter has gone on to unite. Unfortunately, however, one of the screws used to fix the trochanter had backed out and you developed pain and discomfort in your hip as a result of prominence of the screw. The screw was removed. As a result, you have had significant pain directly over the lateral aspect of your hip. The hardware still remains in the hip and does not have to be removed.

It is my feeling that your trochanter will go on to heal.

Regarding the results of Hermann's knee surgery, the doctor indicated that he had a tear in his meniscus [cartilage], which was removed with arthroscopic surgery. This, it was hoped, would provide Hermann some relief from the pain, but the doctor warned Hermann that he now had an increased risk for the development of osteoarthritis in the knee and gave him a "50 percent chance of having significant arthritis within twenty years."

On August 10, 1995, the Crown's appeal against Hermann Beier's sentence was heard by a panel of judges: Justice John Brooke, Justice Patrick Galligan, and Madame Justice Karen Weiler. The Crown, represented by Christine Bartlett-Hughes, sought the addition of three years to Hermann's sentence, from fifteen years (less two years for previous time served) to eighteen years.

Hermann's lawyer, Brian Greenspan, argued for close to an hour — a significant increase from the standard fifteen minutes generally set down for appeals, said Sharon Lavine, a lawyer in Greenspan's Toronto office.

The result, brought in at 1:30 p.m., was a unanimous dismissal of the appeal, which was good news for Hermann. An Endorsement, the reason for the dismissal, was drawn up and signed by the three justices:

If this case had gone to trial and the respondent had been convicted of all or most of these charges, sentences totalling substantially more than those imposed by the trial judge might well have been upheld. However, the totality in this case must be looked at from the context of all the circumstances which were considered by the trial judge.

There had been numerous and protracted pre-trial conferences, the trial judge conducted a number of them, including the crucial one. The respondent's guilty pleas saved the state a tremendous expenditure of resources that would have been necessary if all these charges were to be tried. The pleas also ensured convictions on some of the charges that might not have been open and shut. The case was a unique one, both in its circumstances and in the efforts that were made to resolve it. The trial judge was acutely aware of all of its essential features. He arrived at a result which he thought was an appropriate balance between the need for denunciation for the respondent's conduct, general and specific deterrence, and the protection of the public on the one hand, and both the rehabilitation of the respondent and the very substantial saving of resources of the state on the other.

In the exceptional circumstances of this case, we cannot say that the totality of the sentences indicates an error in principle. Nor can we say that the sentences in their totality were unfit. The application for leave to appeal sentence is granted, the appeal therefrom is dismissed.

The short explanation? Hermann saved the system quite a bit of money by pleading guilty (despite some of his earlier misgivings about doing so) and so was rewarded with not having extra time added to his stay. It turned out Paul Stern's advice at the start was good advice, after all.

In a telephone interview shortly after the appeal, Brian Greenspan said this was an unusual case. "What was unusual about this was that the Crown's appeal was taking place despite the fact that the sentence imposed was known in advance," he said. "Normally, it's when you walk away disappointed one way or another [that an appeal is sought]. It's usually on the basis that you don't know what sentence it is in advance of what the judge is going to impose."

Knowing the sentence beforehand, the Crown had an opportunity to ask for another judge before the sentence was brought down. Why the Crown opted to wait until after the sentence is a mystery, he said.

Crown lawyers were unavailable for comment.

Greenspan told me that with the appeal behind him, Hermann could continue to serve out his sentence in relative peace.

"It's over," he said. "It's finished. Mr. Beier now has a fixed sentence and will, subject to earned remission and parole, serve out his remaining term of the thirteen-year sentence."

25

ENDPOINT

By 1996, Hermann Beier didn't hear much from his friends anymore. Kathleen hadn't contacted him "in a long time," he told me in a letter, but left it at that. His sisters still wrote to him though; they told him how they had spent the past summer, of trips to Wasaga Beach, of life's trials and joys beyond the concrete walls and razor-wire fences.

Hermann's time was spent working at the institution, planning his lawsuit against Corrections Canada and the police, exercising with his Chinese friend, as he called him, and cooking his own food (a necessity due to his sensitive stomach).

Hermann would serve out the rest of his sentence in relative peace. His wife would continue working at a Tim Hortons in Kingston, where she had already been promoted to shift manager. He continued to write to me, but the intervals became longer.

Even as the security at the Joyceville Institution tightened, as more inmates died of overdoses, as more guards allegedly pilfered food and blamed it on the inmates — amid all of the controversy and the hatred and the cacophony of anger and hostility that rang throughout its hallways, there would be one inmate in Joyceville who would sleep peacefully. Having forgiven himself for the crimes he committed, he had finally made peace with the world. And it appeared fairly certain that when Inmate Beier made his exit from Joyceville, he would make damn sure that he wouldn't be returning.

§

The town of Bobcaygeon, often called the "Hub of the Kawarthas," sits just north of Lindsay, Ontario. It is an area of gently rolling hills covered with maple trees, evergreens, and farmer's fields dotted with black and white herds of Holstein cattle, and intersected by rambling streams that babble and bubble their way through the Trent River system. It's as well-known for its streams and rivers, with their smallmouth bass and walleye fishing, and its cottages that hug the shorelines of the lakes surrounding it, as it is for the smiles on the faces of its townsfolk. The downtown is lined with quaint shops. It's one of those genuine places that still appear unsullied by tourism, and this town of 3,500 has so far avoided becoming a tourist trap.

This is where I found Hermann Beier, now in his early sixties, his face red from the sun. He was jovial, smiling, and full of good cheer. It was 2004, and though we had maintained correspondence via mail and later email, it had been seven years since I had last seen him. His tummy was ample and pushed gently at the seams of his cotton work shirt, but he still carried himself with the broad-shouldered confidence that had prompted hard-edged inmates to stay away while he was in the prison system. Sporting an earring on each lobe (still the old hipster), hair the colour of bleached cotton, and a goatee, his visage was arresting the first time I saw him. I noticed a slight strain in his walk, though — likely arthritis settling into his bones. But he certainly looked as if he belonged there, as if he, like others, was an escapee from the urban hustle-and-bustle, running away to a village where no one asked questions, where you could work with your hands, and where the sound of the Trent Severn Waterway rushing down to Lake Ontario provided a rapid, percussive background beat; at this time in the early spring, it was perhaps the only fast-moving thing in town.

Hermann had been out of the prison system for nearly five years. Sometime before his release, his wife had left him. He wasn't dwelling on it. "That's life," he told me, but offered no more. He had finished serving his time in Joyceville, then spent a year at a minimum-security "camp" called Frontenac, near Collins Bay Penitentiary, getting ready to be integrated back into society; after that it was off to a halfway house in Peterborough in 1998, living with others who were also finishing their time. His parole was to continue until 2006, and he wouldn't be completely unsupervised until then. By that time it would be thirteen years since he was first sentenced.

Hermann moved to Bobcaygeon after his time in the halfway house, but he told me he wouldn't be there for long — he had accepted a position with a religious camp near Barrie that was run by a Latvian church organization. He had been hired to look after the grounds.

He paused to lift his shirt, revealing a long scar, the result of his latest operation, this one to repair his digestive system. It looked hardened and dense, a milky-pale tributary springing from a source on his lower trunk and meandering north before petering out at his rib cage, a mark committed to memory and maybe the starting point of a story or two. It was one of many scars.

Hermann's apartment was in a two-storey addition built onto the back of a jewellery store, and accessible by a quaint laneway around back. The living room was warm, and showcased touches of work done by Hermann; cottagey wood paneling and other rural design elements had been added to dress it up.

Hermann's love for animals had been rekindled after his release. By the front door, a wooden aviary held a collection of budgies, all chattering away with one another and hopping from perch to perch. A large sheepdog padded through the house, and there was a large aquarium along one wall and a dish of pet turtles.

He had a girlfriend, too, a woman named Angela. She was blonde, quietly strong and enthusiastic, quite a few years younger than Hermann, and she appeared to me to be the kind of staunch life-supporter Hermann needed. They'd been together for three years. It was actually her apartment, and she had invited Hermann to move in. Angela worked in a quaint little bookstore tucked into an old stone building on the main street, and just a short walk from the apartment. The store sold novels, magazines, new age publications, and self-help and local history books. She was bubbly and seemed committed to Hermann, but at the same time she came across as a no-nonsense kind of woman: she knew what he was about, knew the path he'd travelled.

Hermann told me that nobody in Bobcaygeon had asked about his background. They simply saw him for what essentially he was: an older man coming to town for a second, maybe a third chance. "But I [would] only tell them if they ask me," he added.

"Since I'm here, it takes some time for people to get to know me. But now everybody knows me. I do some grass cutting and odd jobs. I don't do so much woodworking anymore. I can't lift the way I could. Three years ago somebody hired me for grass cutting and so I do that — and snow blowing in the wintertime. And security for houses, over the winter … checking on their houses to be sure they're safe."

About his new employment opportunity at the religious camp, Hermann told me he would be "totally in charge of everything, from reservations to cleaning up — everything."

He told me his family still had mixed feelings about him. He rarely talked to his sisters, but he had gone to Germany to see his kids two years earlier. His grandchildren were growing fast, and he would soon become a great-grandfather — his oldest grandson was already twenty-six years old. Before that trip, Hermann hadn't seen his children since 1991, when he had spent four days back home after the death of his father.

When I asked him about prison, Hermann told me that he didn't keep in touch with any of his fellow inmates. "That's against the rules. And I don't want anything to do with it. I don't want to go back."

As he carefully prepared a pot of brewed coffee at the small white stove in the kitchen, Hermann reflected on the strength of mind and spirit that had carried him during those years. The birds' chatter in the entry hall made me think of the pops and whistles of an old-time calliope.

Hermann recounted his time in prison. "First of all, you learn the system," he said. "You learn the way to respect the guards. I learned what my father went through when he was a guard in Germany. Myself, I learned a lot on my own. Not so much from anger management, but from the courses you take, you learn for yourself. When you have the time and open up, you learn what's wrong with you. You realize what's going on with you. There are a lot of positives. It's funny what you learn in a prison. It doesn't matter what you do, crime is crime and crime never pays off. You learn from it. You learn to cope from the environment.

"The best way to cope is to think like you're in the military. You wear some type of uniform; you're up in the morning, you go to the toilet, you go to meals, you go somewhere, always controlled. You realize that respect for the guards is important. You realize, you give them respect and then get respect back."

Bobcaygeon, 2004. Hermann steered clear of trouble following his release, and had found a new love. He was preparing for a new life working as both a caretaker at a religious camp and as a handyman.

Now he was preparing for the move further west, and he and Angela planned to settle down to work for the religious group for a few years before he would be able to retire. He told me he wanted to travel when he retired, "two to three times a year. I want to see something of North America. I'm not so crazy about going home again."

§

I remember making the trip to Wasaga Beach many years ago. If you lived in the Greater Toronto Area, it was an ideal weekend destination, a great place to go with friends — cheap and relaxed and easy to reach. In those days the roads were rough, gravelly, and I made the drive in my 1969 Chevy Malibu — a real beater, but with nice lines (but certainly no El Dorado). I would travel up Highway 400, then to Highway 26, and continue north. Getting to the beach was the goal — it's still advertised as the longest freshwater beach in the world — and it was a great place to spend a day or two wiling away the time watching the waves of

Georgian Bay roll in, or wandering through the arcades, greasy snack stands, and beach shops.

Much has changed since then. The roads are better, and the town is much bigger. Beach shops and burger joints have been joined by big name retailers and huge grocery stores, and the area is now home to scores of condominiums that people live in year-round. Much has changed, but, like a tip of the hat to its roots, much has also stayed the same. Rustic cottages are still available to rent, and the "surf shacks" continue to hug the promenade along the beach, selling T-shirts, Day-Glo beach towels, and kitsch.

It's now 2009, and in these early days of May, the stores are brimming with merchandise, getting ready for the big "May 2-4" weekend. I'm heading to one of the area's many trailer parks to see Hermann. It's been five years since I last visited him in Bobcaygeon.

My old Chevy Malibu is long gone, and instead I drive a late-model Honda Accord. Where in the past I would rely on landmarks and memory (left turn on Highway 26, right turn on Mosley Street), the way to Hermann's home is clearly marked on the Google map sitting on my front seat.

Hermann Beier is now just shy of his sixty-eighth birthday. He lives and works as a maintenance man in the trailer park, which is located off a main road, seven kilometres from Wasaga's main drag. He's only been living here for a couple of months.

When I arrive, I'm uncertain whether the trailer park has seen better days or if it has always been this way — looking a little worn around the edges, a faded patch of grass and trees and trailer sites. But it looks comfortable, and I can imagine people setting up their trailers here year after year, building a fire at night in an open pit, roasting marshmallows, having a barbeque, opening up a case of beer (saving the hard stuff for later in the evening), and thinking about nothing much except what to do that day and the next.

Just inside the entrance to the park, past the wood-slab forest ranger gates, is the office, an older building made of concrete and brick. It looks as if someone has recently tried to brighten it up with a fresh coat of paint. Across a lawn invaded by crabgrass sits a square concrete building, which houses washrooms and showers for the campers,

As the handyman and jack-of-all-trades at a Wasaga Beach trailer park in 2009, Hermann, single again after breaking up with his live-in girlfriend, was eking out a living.

and a playground with a rough-hewn climbing apparatus, swings, and several big tractor tires half-buried in the dirt. Robins make erratic stop-and-start dashes around the edge of the playground, searching for worms and grubs. Children clamber over the slides and the playground equipment, laughing.

Hermann is in the front office. He sees my car and walks across a grassy patch of ground with tight, short strides. His hair is still snow white. He has a goatee that, in a passing glance, makes him look to me just a little bit like hockey icon Don Cherry. His eyeglasses are frameless and modern-looking. He wears all black — black jeans, black boots, a black jacket with crosses embroidered on the epaulets, and a black cowboy hat. Around his neck hang two silver crucifixes. He is a Lutheran now, he tells me, and although there is not a Lutheran church in Wasaga Beach, he is hopeful that at some point, as the town grows bigger, a Lutheran church will be built. He hasn't changed much in the past five years — he's still stocky, and he walks with a robust strength and authority.

Hermann has an electric cart that carries him around the trailer park. The back is filled with equipment and boxes, the stuff of a handyman and jack-of-all-trades. The trip up to his trailer site is across a dirt path pocked with small muddy holes brimming with water from a recent rainfall. Hermann's old trailer, purchased from his sister, sits on concrete blocks. There's a picnic table out front. The step to get into the trailer — like the majority of trailers, you enter through a sliding glass door — is a concrete block with two holes in the middle (what is called in the construction trade a stretcher block). The area in front of the trailer has been cleared of whatever grass or weeds once grew there and the earth has been levelled. Hermann has put four stakes into the earth, approximating the dimensions of a rectangle, maybe five feet by twelve feet, and string has been pulled taut between the stakes — he tells me this is in preparation for the deck he is planning to build.

He has no wife, no girlfriend now, and he has a look of tired resignation when he mentions this. Perhaps he has had enough of women (although he doesn't say this, I get that feeling from the look on his face). Perhaps he is just tired of relationships. In 2004, he and his girlfriend from Bobcaygeon had moved to the religious camp near Barrie, and he worked there for a year. But it wasn't a good situation, he tells me. Angela missed Bobcaygeon and decided to move back. Hermann then moved to Honey Harbour and stayed there until he left for Germany the previous winter. He had spent five months in Europe, visiting with his children, grandchildren, and great-grandchildren. He has lived at the trailer park since returning to Canada in March.

The trailer is cramped. Boxes of food, clothing, and assorted items are arranged in ordered chaos about the place. He is still unpacking. There is a bedroom at one end and a small washroom at the other. The kitchen area is opposite the door, and a small, firm couch offers a place to sit. Near the door, a TV sits on a small stand. Stacked on the couch at one end is a collection of DVDs, and I notice *The Bourne Identity* on top. Slightly off-centre is a sitting area; a small table that sticks out from the wall provides an all-purpose surface for breakfast, lunch, or dinner. A hotplate sits on the counter. There are boxes of cereals and containers of pasta and other food. Hermann drinks a green liquid from a clear plastic bottle. It's for his health, he says, a seaweed and herb concoction from a health food store. He needs another operation on his hip, he says, and he wants to lose some weight before he goes under the knife.

He spends his days looking after the campsite. Every once in a while someone comes to the door and raps quickly on it. They want him to fix small things mostly: a repair to a picnic table; a clogged toilet; the occasional fallen tree branch that needs to be cleared away from a campsite. Hermann is polite, firm, and professional; he makes a note, and tells them he has guests but will be there momentarily.

Things did not turn out the way he hoped they would, but it doesn't matter now, he says. "You just live each day the way it comes." We talk about the mundane, run-of-the-mill, day-to-day things.

I have brought my younger son, Cole, with me to meet Hermann. He and my other kids had heard me talk about Hermann over the years, had seen me writing out notes from visits and compiling photographs and putting together the book, and he was curious to see what this former bank robber would look like. I think he's a little surprised that Hermann isn't a big, brash, hard-as-nails tough guy like the movie bank robbers; instead he is reserved, even gentle. The term *grandfatherly* comes to mind.

As we prepare to leave, after my son gets into the car, Hermann nods toward him and asks me quietly, "So he knows about me, what I did, eh?" There is just the slightest hint of embarrassment in his voice; he still wants to be respected, understood by young people. I tell Hermann that yes, I had told Cole about him, but I explain that he also understands that after a person serves their time, they are free to live their life. Hermann smiles slightly, relieved perhaps. "That is good."

As we drive away, I watch him move toward the office. He will go about his life here. No more harlequin budgies, no more dreams of glory. Just time. And working with his hands.

Postscript

Hermann Beier

In 2010, Hermann started visiting Germany and Austria more often. He has reconnected with his family, which now includes many grandchildren and great-grandchildren. And he fell in love. He now lives with his girlfriend in Graz, Austria, a city with a population of just under 300,000. He is retired, his health is good, and he lives on the small amount of pension money that he receives, including from his Canada Pension Plan, and divides his time between Austria and Canada.

Al Stennett

As of the publication date, Al Stennett continues to serve with the Halton Regional Police Service — the same force that he joined in 1982. He received his thirty-year Police Exemplary Service Medal from the Governor General of Canada's office in February 2013. Following the chase that resulted in Hermann Beier's arrest, he received a Chief's Letter of Recognition in 1992, a Police Association Award of Excellence, and was honoured as The Optimist Club of Georgetown's Officer of the Year for 1991. In 1995, he transferred from the role of patrol office to the then-regional traffic bureau, and founded the Halton Police Service's Commercial Vehicle Enforcement Unit in 2002; eight years later he created and chaired the Ontario Police Commercial Vehicle Committee. In 2008, he received a lifetime achievement award for his work in traffic safety from the Ontario Association of Chiefs of Police and was a recipient of a Silver Jubilee Award from the Halton Regional Police Service for his long-term efforts in traffic safety.

Paul Stern

Hermann Beier's lawyer continues to run a busy practice in downtown Toronto, now called Stern Landesman Clarke LLP. He has provided counsel for administrative tribunals, and has represented clients in provincial courts outside Ontario, at all levels of the justice system in Ontario, and before the Supreme Court of Canada.

Changes in Police Services

The following changes in police services were implemented following the chase and takedown of Hermann Beier:

- officers were issued semi-automatic pistols;
- more police forces implemented the use of police helicopters, which were very effective in tracking Hermann's movements during the chase and providing vital information about his location to officers on the ground;
- the number of shotguns in police patrol vehicles was increased (previously restricted mainly to supervisors' vehicles);
- new and more comprehensive approaches to the issue of Post-Traumatic Stress Disorder and its treatment through police Employee Assistance Programs, as well as the way in which police forces generally manage *all* cases of post-crisis stress.

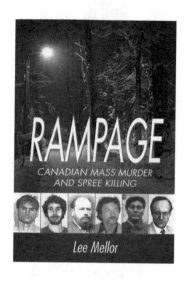

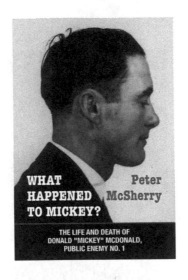

What Happened to Mickey?
The Life and Death of Donald "Mickey" McDonald, Public Enemy No. 1
by Peter McSherry
9781459707382
$24.99

Donald "Mickey" McDonald was charged in 1939 with the killing of a bookmaker, supposedly Toronto's first gangland slaying. Two murder trials, a sensational escape from Kingston Penitentiary, and a $50,000 bank robbery established Mickey as a national crime figure, though the circumstances of his death still remain mysterious.

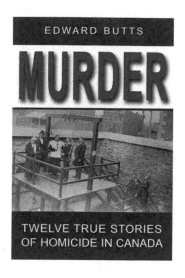

Murder
Twelve True Stories of Homicide in Canada
by Edward Butts
9781554887620
$24.99

Who committed Toronto's Silk Stocking Murder? Why did a quiet accountant in Guelph, Ontario, murder his wife and two daughters? When did police in Alberta hire a self-styled mind reader to solve a mass murder? How did an American confidence man from Arizona find himself facing a murder charge in Cape Breton, Nova Scotia? These questions and more are answered in *Murder: Twelve True Stories of Homicide in Canada*, the latest collection of thrilling true Canadian crime stories by Edward Butts.

The keenly researched chapters tell the stories behind some of Canada's most fascinating murder cases, from colonial times to the twentieth century, and from the Atlantic provinces to the West Coast and up to the Arctic.

⛫DUNDURN

Visit us at
Definingcanada.ca
@dundurnpress
Facebook.com/dundurnpress

MIX
Paper from
responsible sources
FSC® C004071